MUSIC FROM SCRATCH

A music course for CSE

Tony Attwood

Dartington College of Arts

Oxford University Press

Music Department
Ely House, 37 Dover Street, London W1X 4AH

First published 1980

ISBN 0 19 321020 7

Filmset and printed in Great Britain by
BAS Printers Limited, Over Wallop, Hampshire

ACKNOWLEDGEMENTS

Photographs
Page 54 (*top*) Foto R. de Voeght, (*bottom left*), The British Library,
(*bottom right*) Mansell Collection; p. 56 Mansell Collection; p. 57
Bildarchiv der Öst Nationalbibliothek; p. 58 Mansell Collection; p. 59
(*top*) Jean Loup Charmet, (*bottom*) Ferdinandeum Museum, Innsbruck;
p. 60 Walter Danz; p. 64–5 Hulton Picture Library; p. 66 Bildarchiv
der Öst Nationalbibliothek; p. 67 Hulton Picture Library; p. 70 (*left*)
Archiv für Kunst und Geschichte, Berlin; p. 76 Hulton Picture Library;
p. 77 Hulton Picture Library; p. 78 (*left*) Bibliothèque Nationale, Paris,
(*right*) Mansell Collection; p. 82 Hulton Picture Library; p. 83 Mansell
Collection; p. 84 (*top left*) Archiv für Kunst und Geschichte, Berlin (*top
right*) Hulton Picture Library, (*bottom*) Richard Macnutt Collection; p.
87 Hulton Picture Library, (*bottom*) Richard Macnutt Collection; p. 87
Hulton Picture Library; p. 88 Hulton Picture Library; p. 89 (*left*)
Hulton Picture Library, (*right*) Mansell Collection; p. 80 Boosey &
Hawkes; p. 95 Report, photo Patrick Eagar; p. 96 Report, photo Peter
Harrap; p. 98 (*top*) Nigel Luckhurst, (*bottom*) Camera Press; p. 101–2
Keystone Press; p. 103 Camera Press; p. 104 David Redfern; p. 108
(*bottom*) Mansell Collection; p. 111 (*top*) Finlandia Kuva Oy, Helsinki.

Drawings Constance Dear.

Author's note
I should like to thank Peter Collis, Howard Rees and Peter West of the
Cockpit Arts Workshop, London, for their invaluable help in preparing
this book.

Contents

Foreword

Music from scratch is a textbook for use with secondary students who approach C.S.E. or O level music with little or no musical background. It assumes no musical knowledge at all, and is designed to present the relevant information to the students, and then test this information with exercises and questions. The student is thus allowed to work at his or her own speed.

The book consists of four sections – the first covers the harmony and melody writing aspect of C.S.E. music courses, taking the student from the meaning of the treble clef to two-part harmony and eight-bar melodies. Section 2 covers the history of music from the 16th century to the advent of the avant-garde and popular music – particular care being taken here to describe not only the development of pop but also to relate it to the development of contemporary music that springs from the 'classical-romantic' tradition. This section also contains the most important features of the life and work of 22 major composers set out in tabulated form, enabling the student to look up this information quickly.

Section 3 briefly describes the appearance, function and sound of the main instruments found in the orchestra, pop group and electronic studio, whilst section 4 sets out definitions of musical terms relating to form, dynamics etc., that the student will be expected to know for a C.S.E. music exam. It is felt that these two sections will be particularly useful to the student who needs to find out basic facts very quickly.

The book has been designed to cover all the main features of the syllabuses of the various C.S.E. Boards, except for the set works, for which the history component of this book will give the sort of background knowledge of music that examiners often require when testing awareness of the context of the set works. In order to help the teacher give the students direct musical experience a number of records are recommended throughout section 2.

Tony Attwood, 1980

SECTION 1

Harmony and tune-writing

Note to the teacher

Some teachers may be a little surprised at the order in which material is presented in this section of the book. Traditionally, the student of musical notation has been asked to learn a large number of rules and regulations before tackling his first piece of creative writing in the form of a tune. Here, however, tune-writing is introduced at a very early stage, in a rather formalized way. Other items, traditionally introduced early in a course, are left until later.

This method of working is the result of two years' experimentation and research at Aylestone High School and William Forster School in North London. The aim was to find a way of giving students a greater sense of purpose when learning the rules of musical notation, so that this in turn would encourage the students and enable them to relate the theory more rapidly to the sound of music rather than seeing it as a series of abstract mathematical principles. This aim was achieved most satisfactorily when tune-writing was introduced very early on, providing the students were given every opportunity and encouragement to hear and play each other's music.

One further point needs to be added, on the question of what is included, and what is not. There are currently 13 separate examination bodies in England administering their own C.S.E. music exams. Separate bodies also exist in Wales, Scotland and Northern Ireland. In addition, many teachers are now working on mode 3 C.S.E. syllabuses which often differ quite dramatically from the mode 1 syllabuses. With such diversity it is impossible to produce a textbook that covers everything. Thus, the aim here has been to cover the basic ground. Towards the end of this section of the book some topics are introduced which may need expansion for some syllabuses, whilst others may be omitted altogether. Nevertheless, teachers should find that all the groundwork that is needed is given here. Those pupils who come to a C.S.E. or O level class with some musical knowledge can work their way through the exercises of the book, turning back to the text at any exercise they are unable to answer. Students coming to the subject for the first time should find the text complete in itself and usable both in class and for homework. Upon completion, students should be able to tackle not only the theory examination papers at C.S.E. level, but also the optional project work that appears on many syllabuses in which students are invited to write their own music on a firm chordal basis.

Introduction

Although a few contemporary composers have found it necessary to invent new forms of musical notation, most write down their music in a standard way that has been developed over hundreds of years. It is this method that you will learn about in this section of the book.

1. Notes

EXAMPLE 1

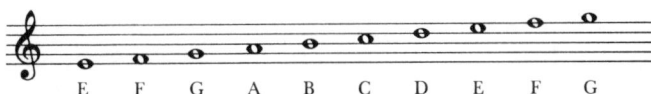

E F G A B C D E F G

In this method music is written on a five-line grid (called a STAVE), with the notes written on the lines and in the spaces between the lines. Sometimes, as you will see, they are also written just above the five-line stave.

In example 1 you can see that there is a sign written on the left of the notes, and then the ten notes with their names written underneath. The sign on the left is a TREBLE CLEF. It's an important sign as it tells the musician that the names of the notes will be as shown in example 1. (There is also a clef called a BASS CLEF which gives the notes different names. You will learn about this on page 33. But for now concentrate on the treble clef.)

Exercise 1a It is important that you should be able to draw a treble clef. Practise drawing one until you have got it right. Draw it in three stages. First, the line from the bottom upwards:

Next, bring the line over to the right and curl it down to the left:

Finally, add the bottom curl:

Exercise 1b *Draw the treble clef and write in the four notes F A C E, using the E that is the furthest to the right in example 1.*

Exercise 1c *Draw the treble clef and write in the five notes E G B D F. This time use the E and G that are furthest to the left and the F that is furthest to the right.*

You should have found that in exercise 1b all the notes were in spaces and in exercise 1c they were on the lines. You will notice that in example 1 there is more than one of the notes E F and G. This is because the notes form a pattern which is repeated after seven steps up or down. Hence only the letters A to G (seven letters in all) need to be used. The higher a note is written on the five lines, the higher it sounds, so the G on the right is higher than the G on the left.

7

EXAMPLE 2

Exercise 2a Look at the notes written in example 2. Write down the words that the notes spell.

Exercise 2b *Now draw the following words as notes on a five-line stave. Put a treble clef before you start each word:*

i) DAD ii) CAB iii) CABBAGE iv) CAGE v) BAD vi) FAB vii) CAFE

Don't forget that whenever you have an E, an F, or a G, you have two notes to choose from – a high one and a low one. You can choose whichever one you like.

EXAMPLE 3

Chords of C major

It is possible to put two or more notes together. When there are more than two we have a CHORD. Example 3 shows three notes together – C E and G with a treble clef in front of them. When these three notes are written together the chord is known as the chord of C major.

In order to write a chord of C major it does not matter which order the three notes come in – you could put the G at the bottom if you wanted to, as in the second example. As long as the three notes are C E and G, the chord is known as the chord of C major.

Exercise 3 *Draw a chord of C major, with a treble clef in front of it. Choose one that is different from the examples, if you can.*

EXAMPLE 4

Chord of F major   Chord of G major

Example 4 shows two more chords, the chord of F major (with the notes F A and C) and next to that the chord of G major (the notes are G B and D).

Exercise 4a *Draw a treble clef with a chord of G major after it, followed by a chord of F major. (Choose 'note arrangements' that are different from the examples.)*

Exercise 4b *Answer the following questions:*
   i) Which chord uses the note F?
   ii) Which chords use the note C?
   iii) Which chord uses the note D?
   iv) Which chords use the note G?

DON'T FORGET TO PLAY ALL THE EXAMPLES AND EXERCISES

2. Rhythm

a) Crotchets (quarter notes)

EXAMPLE 5

Notes can be either long or short. Example 5 shows a short note. It is an E that is filled in and has a stem. It is called a CROTCHET. In America it is called a QUARTER NOTE.

Exercise 5   *Draw a treble clef and a crotchet E.*

EXAMPLE 6

E   F   G   A   B   C   D   E   F   G

Example 6 shows all the notes you met in example 1, but now drawn as crotchets. You can see that the stems of the five notes on the left (low E to B) go up from the head, and join the head on its right. In all the other notes the stems go down and join the head on its left. In fact the stem of B can go either up or down – here it has been drawn going up.

Exercise 6   *Draw the following words as crotchets. Put a treble clef before each word:*
a) EGG b) CABBAGE c) DEAD d) BADGE e) FACE f) BEEF

b) Minims (half notes)

EXAMPLE 7

If we want a note that is longer than a crotchet we can draw a note that still has a stem but is not filled in. It is called a MINIM, or in America, a HALF NOTE. Example 7 shows a minim C.

Exercise 7   *Now you've seen a minim C, draw all the notes shown in example 6, but make them minims. This means you must first draw the treble clef and then the ten notes from low E to high G. Don't forget to make the stems go the right way.*

c) Bar lines

EXAMPLE 8

Example 8 shows four crotchets followed by a line. The line is called a BAR LINE.

Exercise 8   *Write down the letter names of the crotchets in example 8.*

9

d) Time: $\frac{4}{4}$

EXAMPLE 9

Notice the sign of two 4s, one over the other in example 9. Notice also that after the last bar there is a DOUBLE BAR LINE. This shows that we have reached the end.

You can see that in bar 1 there are four crotchets, in bar 2 there are two minims, in bar 3 there are four crotchets again, and in the fourth bar there are two minims.

Each of these four bars has the same number of beats in it. That means that if you were to count a steady beat, say once a second, the same number of seconds would pass by in the playing of bar 1 as bar 2, even though bar 2 only has two notes in it. The reason is simple. 1 minim = 2 crotchets. Thus all the bars have four crotchets worth of beats in them.

Exercise 9a   *Look at example 9 and answer these questions.*
i) In bar 1 how many crotchets are there?
ii) In bar 2 there are two minims – how many crotchets does each minim equal?
iii) How many minims are there in bar 3?
iv) What are the letter names of the notes in bar 4?

The time signature ($\frac{4}{4}$) written at the start of this piece of music tells us that there will be four crotchet beats in each bar. The top number says there will be four beats, and the bottom number means that they will be crotchets. So if the time signature was $\frac{3}{4}$ it would mean that there would be three crotchet beats in each bar.

Exercise 9b   *i) What does a time signature tell you?*
ii) What does the time signature $\frac{4}{4}$ mean?
iii) If you saw a time signature that read $\frac{2}{4}$ what would that mean?

e) Semibreves (whole notes)

EXAMPLE 10

There is a note even longer than a minim called a SEMIBREVE (or in America a WHOLE NOTE). This is the longest note in common use in music today. It is equal to two minims, or four crotchets. So in a piece of music that has the time signature $\frac{4}{4}$ it is possible to write a bar that contains four crotchets, or two minims, or just one semibreve. Example 10 shows all these possibilities.

Exercise 10   *Complete the following sentences which refer to example 10.*
The music starts with a treble _____. After that comes $\frac{4}{4}$ which is a time _____. It means there are 4 _____ in each bar. In the first bar there are two _____. In the last bar there is one _____. At the end of the piece, after the last note, there is a

_____ _____ _____.

EXAMPLE 11

Example 11 shows how a semibreve relates to a minim and how they both relate to a crotchet.

10

3. Four-bar tunes

EXAMPLE 12

C E G   F A C   G B D

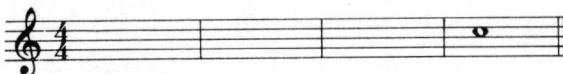

Example 12 has four bars. In the last bar a note has been written in (a semibreve C), but the other three bars have yet to be completed. You have to complete the other three bars and write a short tune. Afterwards, try and play it on a piano, glockenspiel or other keyboard instrument, or perhaps your teacher will play it for you. To help you to decide which notes to use a choice of notes has been put above each bar. You will see that they are taken from the three chords that were shown in examples 3 and 4. Now look at exercise 12.

Exercise 12   *Draw a treble clef and time signature and write down the notes, with their letter names above, to fill in the empty bars.*

EXAMPLE 13

Example 13 shows another slightly different way of writing this four-bar tune. As you can see, any of the notes can be repeated in each bar. Also, you can use minims and crotchets in any way you like in the first three bars, as long as the total number of crotchet beats always adds up to four beats per bar.

Exercise 13a   *Complete the outline tune shown in example 12 in a different way from that shown in example 13.*

Exercise 13b   *Just to check you've fully understood what is required in writing this four-bar tune, write another tune in the same way and fill in the table below.*

Bar	Notes which can be used	Notes actually used
1	C E G	— — — —
2	F A C	— — — —
3	G B D	— — — —
4	C	C

Exercise 13c   *Explain the meaning of the following terms:*
i)   *time signature*
ii) *bar line*
iii) *chord of F major*
iv) *crotchet*
v) *semibreve*
vi *double bar line*

4. Notes (continued)

a) Leger lines

EXAMPLE 14

? ? E F G A B C D E F G

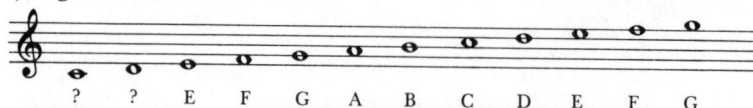

Some notes that we have not used before have been added to the list of notes available. The notes continue to be named in alphabetical order, so the two low notes are C and D. You will see that the lowest note of all is drawn below the five lines and has a line drawn through the middle of it. This little line is just like a sixth line, and it is in fact possible to add extra lines above and below the stave, for notes that are higher or lower. These extra lines are called LEGER LINES.

Exercise 14   *Copy out example 14, but draw all the notes as crotchets and write in the names of the two notes that have been given question marks in the example.*

EXAMPLE 15

Here are some more notes written above or below the stave.

Exercise 15   *Look at example 15 and work out the names of the notes that do not have their names written in. Remember you simply have to keep going in alphabetical order from A to G, and then start again at A.*

b) The piano keyboard

EXAMPLE 16

C D E F G A B C D E F G

C D E F G A B C D E F G

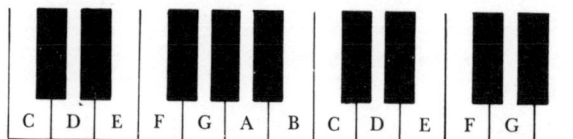

You may find it helpful to try out the tunes you write on a piano, or other keyboard instrument. To help you, the names of the notes found on a piano, glockenspiel or xylophone have been written in, with the actual notes written underneath.

Exercise 16   *Which is the lowest note shown on the piano in example 16?*

DON'T FORGET TO PLAY ALL THE EXAMPLES AND EXERCISES

5. Sharps

In example 16 some of the notes (the smaller ones) are shaded in. On the piano they are coloured black. Example 17 shows the names of these notes.

EXAMPLE 17

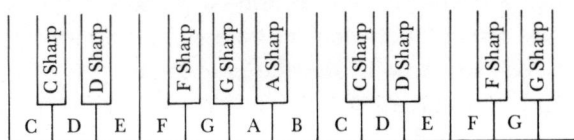

Exercise 17a   Copy out the piano keyboard as in example 16, and write in the names of the black notes.

Exercise 17b   Remember that the further a note is to the right on a piano keyboard the higher it is. Complete the following:
C sharp is higher than C but lower than D.
D sharp is _____ than D but lower than _____.
F _____ is _____ than _____ but _____than _____.
G_____.
A _____.

EXAMPLE 18

There is a short way of writing the word SHARP, by putting the special sign ♯ in front of the note. Example 18 shows F sharp and C sharp.

Exercise 18a   Name the following notes.

Exercise 18b   Write the following notes: A sharp; C sharp; D sharp; F sharp; G sharp.

Exercise 18c   You should now be able to draw a piano keyboard and name all the notes (black and white). Below your drawing, draw a five-line stave and a treble clef, and put in all the notes, including the sharps, under the notes on the piano keyboard.

6. The scales of C major and G major

EXAMPLE 19

Scale of C major

Example 19 shows the SCALE OF C MAJOR. As you can see, it starts with the note C and goes up to the note C above it.

Exercise 19a   *Look back to the piano keyboard and look at the notes of the scale of C major. You will see that there is one note between the first two notes of the scale of C major (that is, between C and D there is C sharp).*
Complete the following:
There are two pairs of notes in the scale of C major that do not have a note between them. One pair is E and F. The other pair is ……

The distance between any one note on the piano and the next note to it is called a SEMITONE. The distance between one note and the note after next is a TONE. So the distance between the note D and the note D sharp is a semitone. The distance between D and E is a tone.

Exercise 19b   *i) What is the distance between F and F sharp?*
                ii) What is the distance between E and F?
                iii) What is the distance between B and C?
                iv) What is the distance between F and G?
The scale of C major contains the notes C D E F G A B C, in that order.

Exercise 19c   *What is the distance between C and D? D and E? E and F? F and G? G and A? A and B? B and C?*

You should find the answer reads as follows: tone; tone; semitone; tone; tone; tone; semitone.

All scales known as major scales follow this exact pattern. So even if you didn't know the names of the notes in the scale of C major you could work them out from the pattern of tones and semitones.

EXAMPLE 20

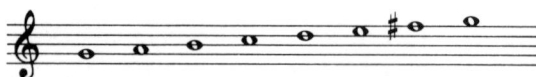

Scale of G major

Example 20 shows the the SCALE OF G MAJOR.

Exercise 20a   *Work out the distance between each note of the scale and the note above it.*
Exercise 20b   *Which pairs of notes have a distance of a semitone between them in the scale of G major?*

7. The keys of C major and G major

EXAMPLE 21

In examples 12 and 13 you were shown how to write a four-bar tune. You'll remember that the tune ended on the note C, and the notes of the tune were selected from the chords of C major, F major and G major. This meant that the only notes used in the tune were notes found in the scale of C major (see example 19).

However, we might want to write a tune that could be played by a certain instrument, or sung by a person with a particular voice range. One way of doing it would be to write the song in a different KEY. The effect of this would be to make all the notes higher (or lower) for the instrument or singer.

All the pieces you have seen so far have been written in the key of C major. Below you will see how to write in the key of G major.

You'll remember that the scale of G major has a sharp in it – F sharp. This means that when writing a piece of music in G major all the Fs will normally be sharp. In order to save writing the sign for a sharp next to each F it is possible to write an F sharp at the start of each line. Example 21 shows how this is done – note that the F sharp is always written on the top line – even though it means that all Fs (including those on the bottom space) are sharp.

An F sharp written at the start of a line of music means that the piece is in the key of G major: in other words, F sharp is the KEY SIGNATURE of G major. In the two earlier tunes there was no key signature because C major contains no sharps.

Exercise 21   a) *What is the key signature of C major?*
b) *What is the key signature of G major?*

EXAMPLE 22

Chord of D major

When you wrote your two tunes earlier both of them had the key signature of C major. If you wanted to write a piece of music in the key of G you would have to write the key signature of G major at the start of the piece. Also you would need to select notes from different chords, to form your tune.

Writing in the key of C major you used the following chords:
Bar 1 used the notes of the chord of C major (C E and G)
Bar 2 used the notes of the chord of F major (F A and C)
Bar 3 used the notes of the chord of G major (G B and D)

Writing in the key of G we can again use the notes of three different chords. Our three chords will be G major (in bar 1), C major (in bar 2) and D major (in bar 3). As before, bar 4 will just have one note – G.

The only new chord is D major, which is shown in example 22. As with all the other chords you have met so far, the chord of D major has three notes: D F sharp and A. However, as the tune will be in the key of G major it will be necessary to write the key signature of G major at the start of the piece, and as this includes an F sharp, it is not necessary to write the sharp next to each F.

Now look at exercise 22.

Exercise 22a   *Fill in the bottom line of the chart.*

KEY	KEY SIGNA-TURE	CHORD FOR BAR 1	NOTES FOR BAR 1	CHORD FOR BAR 2	NOTES FOR BAR 2	CHORD FOR BAR 3	NOTES FOR BAR 3	NOTE FOR BAR 4
G major	F sharp	G major	G B D	C major	C E G	D major	D F sharp A	G
C major	___	___	___	___	___	___	___	___

15

    i) *Draw the key signature of the key of G major.*
    ii) *What are the notes of the chord of G major?*
    iii) *Draw the scale of G major.*
    iv) *What are the three chords used in writing a piece in the key of G major?*

EXAMPLE 23

Example 23 shows a four-bar tune in the key of G major.
Now it is your turn to write a tune in the key of G major.

Exercise 23a   *First draw the treble clef.*
*Now draw the key signature of the key of G major, which is an F sharp on the top line.
The next thing is to put the time signature in, which will be ⁴⁄₄ for this piece of music.
Now mark out the four bars by putting in the bar lines, with a double bar line at the
very end of the piece.*
*Bar 1 has notes in it taken from the chord of G major – these notes are G B and D, so
write the letters G B and D over the first bar.*
*Bar 2 takes notes from the chord of C major – C E and G. Write these letters over the
top of bar 2.*
*Bar 3 takes its notes from the chord of D major – D F sharp and A. Write in these
letters over the top of the third bar.*
    Finally, the fourth bar has just one note – G. Write this over the top of bar 4.
    *Now you simply have to choose which notes to use, making sure you always have
four crotchets worth of notes in each bar. You can use both crotchets and minims, but
do remember that a minim is worth two crotchets. Example 23 shows a completed tune
in the key of G major. Use that as a guide, but don't copy the notes from the example.*

Exercise 23b   *Now write another tune in G major. This time you are given no help at all. If you can't
remember exactly what to do look back to exercise 23a, and example 23.*

EXAMPLE 24

Example 24 shows two tunes, the first in C major and the second in G major. If you
look closely you will find that both songs have the same shape – where one goes up
the other goes up, and so on. In fact, if you check closely you will see that the
shapes are exactly the same except that the song in G is always five SEMITONES
lower than the tune in C.

    Example 24 shows the same tune twice – written first in the key of C major and
secondly in the key of G major. The technical term for rewriting a piece from one
key in another key is TRANSPOSITION. The piece of music in the key of C major has
been *transposed* below into the key of G major. It is in a different key but it is still
the same piece of music.

Exercise 24 a) *When a piece of music is transposed from the key of C major to the key of G major what happens to the key signature?*
b) *When a piece of music is transposed from the key of C major to the key of G major what happens to the time signature?*
c) *If a piece of music in the key of C major is transposed into the key of G major what note will the piece now end on, if it previously ended on a C?*

EXAMPLE 25

Exercise 25 Transpose the piece of music in example 25 down into the key of G major. You may find it helpful to use the following guide.

The note C in the key of C major becomes the note G in the key of G major
The note D in the key of C major becomes the note A in the key of G major
The note E in the key of C major becomes the note B in the key of G major
The note F in the key of C major becomes the note C in the key of G major
The note G in the key of C major becomes the note D in the key of G major
The note A in the key of C major becomes the note E in the key of G major
The note B in the key of C major becomes the note F sharp in the key of G major

8. The key of D major

EXAMPLE 26

Example 26 shows the key signature of a new key, D MAJOR. As you can see, it has the same sharp as in the key signature of G major, plus a new sharp. The two sharps are F sharp and C sharp.

If we write a tune in D major we must put two sharps at the start of each line after the treble clef.

Exercise 26 *Draw the key signatures of a) G major b) C major and c) D major. Remember to put a treble clef before each one.*

EXAMPLE 27

Chord of A major

In the key of C major we used the chords C F and G major when choosing notes for a four-bar tune.

In the key of G major we used the chords G C and D major when choosing notes for a four-bar tune.

Now in the new key of D major we use the chords of D major, G major and A.

major. You already know the chords of D and G major. Example 27 shows the chord of A major. You will see that it has a C sharp in it. It is not necessary to draw it in when writing each C in a tune in the key of D major, as the C sharp is already in the key signature.

Exercise 27 Complete the following.
The chord of C major has three notes which are ......
The chord of D major has three notes which are ......
The chord of F major has three notes which are ......
The chord of G major has three notes which are ......
The chord of A major has three notes which are ......

EXAMPLE 28

When you changed a piece of music from C major into G major you put it in a lower key. If you wanted to change a piece from D major to C major you would again make it lower but this time all you would have to do is move each note down two semitones (that is, one place in the new scale). This means that if you want to move the note D to its equivalent in the key of C major you simply find the note below D in the scale of C major – which of course is C. Example 28 shows a tune in D major transposed into C major.

Exercise 28 Complete the following chart.
The note D in the key of D major = the note C in the key of C major

_____	E _____	=	_____
_____	F sharp _____	=	_____
_____	G _____	=	_____
_____	A _____	=	_____
_____	B _____	=	_____
_____	C sharp _____	=	_____

EXAMPLE 29

Example 29 shows another tune in the key of D major.

Exercise 29a Transpose example 29 into the key of C major. Remember to start with the treble clef, then put the key signature (which in the case of C major is very easy) and then the time signature.

Exercise 29b Write your own tune in D major.[For bar one you must use the notes from the chord of D major (D F sharp or A), for bar two notes from the chord of G major (G B or D) and for bar three notes from the chord of A major (A C sharp or E).]

Exercise 29c Write a tune in C major, but don't use any notes below the F on the bottom space. (The reason is that you will be asked to transpose this tune downwards and if you start

18

off too low down you will be forced to use a large number of notes below the bottom line of your music. But first you are asked to transpose upwards.)

Transpose the tune you have written into the key of D major. Now transpose the tune again into the key of G major. (You may find it easier to go back to your original tune for this rather than trying to transpose the song from D major, although whichever way you do it the result should be the same.)

9. Revision

a) *Fill in the spaces.*
   2 crotchets = 1 ......
   1 semibreve = 2 ...... or 4 ......
b) *Draw a crotchet, a minim and a semibreve.*

10. Rhythm (continued)

a) Quavers (eighth notes)

EXAMPLE 30

The revision was necessary because we are now going to look at another note: the QUAVER (or EIGHTH NOTE). Some quavers are drawn in example 30. If there is just one quaver the stem goes UP if it is below the middle line, and DOWN if it is above the middle line. On the middle line it can go either way. The tail on the end of the stem falls away to the right. If two, three or four quavers come together the tails are then normally all joined together, in the time signatures you have met so far. A quaver is worth half a crotchet. Or to put it another way:
   2 quavers = 1 crotchet
   4 quavers = 2 crotchets or 1 minim
   8 quavers = 4 crotchets or 2 minims or 1 semibreve

Exercise 30   Complete this chart.

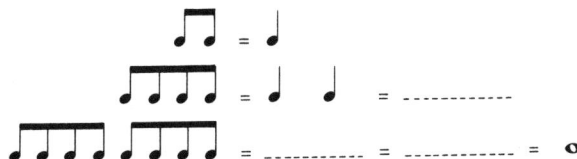

19

EXAMPLE 31

Example 31 shows six bars in 4/4 time. Some of the bars have quaver notes in, others don't.

Exercise 31 *a) How many quaver notes are there in bar 1 ?*
b) How many quaver notes are there in bar 2 ?
c) How many minim notes are there in bar 2 ?
d) How many crotchet notes are there in bar 3 ?
e) How many quaver notes are there in bar 4 ?
f) How many semibreve notes are there in bar 5 ?
g) How many semibreve notes are there in bar 6 ?

EXAMPLE 32

Example 32 shows a tune with some quaver notes in it. You can see the quavers always come together either in pairs, or in fours. Although you will read about individual quavers in a moment, in the exercises that follow, use quavers only in groups of 2 or 4.

Exercise 32a *Write a tune in C major using quavers in at least one bar.*

Exercise 32b *Write a tune in D major using quavers in at least one bar.*

Exercise 32c *Change the tune in exercise 32a into the key of G major.*

b) Dotted notes

EXAMPLE 33

In example 33 you will notice that the third crotchet has a dot after it, and is followed by one quaver on its own. The dot after a note means that the note is worth one and a half times what it would be worth normally. So a dotted crotchet equals one and a half crotchets.

As we know that half a crotchet is a quaver, a dotted crotchet is clearly worth one crotchet and one quaver.

Exercise 33 *Complete the following chart.*

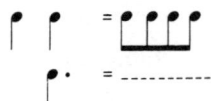

EXAMPLE 34

20

For the moment you should only use the dotted crotchet as shown in example 34 – followed by a quaver. Like almost all the rules in music, this one can be broken sometimes. You will certainly be able to find many pieces of music where it is, but in order to help you understand dotted notes you should stick to the rule for the moment. You will also see that the dotted crotchet and quaver come as a pair on either the first two crotchet beats in a bar of $\frac{4}{4}$ or the last two – not on the second and third beats across the middle of a bar. Again this rule can be broken, but for the moment it is better to remember only to use the crotchet with a dot followed by a quaver as the first two, or last two beats in a bar of $\frac{4}{4}$, as in example 34.

Exercise 34a   *Write a tune in C major, using at least one dotted crotchet in the piece.*

Exercise 34b   *Transpose the tune written in exercise 34a, into D major.*

Exercise 34c   *Write a tune in G major, using at least one dotted crotchet in it.*

EXAMPLE 35

Example 35 shows the dotted minim. Just as a dotted crotchet was worth one and a half crotchets, so a dotted minim is worth one and a half minims. As half a minim is a crotchet, a dotted minim equals one minim and one crotchet.

Exercise 35a   *Complete the following chart.*

Exercise 35b   *Write a four-bar tune in G major, including one dotted minim in it.*

11. More time signatures

EXAMPLE 36

The time signature used so far in this book is $\frac{4}{4}$. This means four crotchets in a bar. However, we can also have music with other time signatures, and in all time signatures the two numbers keep their special meaning:
The *top number* tells the performer the number of beats in a bar.
The *bottom number* tells the performer what kind of beats they are.

As you know, the number 4 at the bottom means crotchet beats – you will remember that the American name for a crotchet is a quarter note. If you write a quarter as a fraction you put the number 4 at the bottom – $\frac{1}{4}$. In music that would mean one quarter beat (or crotchet) in a bar.

Example 36 shows a tune with the time signature of $\frac{3}{4}$. You'll see it uses dotted crotchets in it, but don't think you have to use them when writing in $\frac{3}{4}$! A time signature of $\frac{3}{4}$ will mean three quarter beats (or three crotchets) in a bar. Each bar can have any combination of notes that obeys the rules of music and that totals three crotchet beats. A time signature of $\frac{2}{4}$ will mean two crotchet beats in a bar.

Exercise 36a   *Write a piece of music in $\frac{3}{4}$ time in the key of C major.*

Exercise 36b   *Transpose the piece written for exercise 36a into G major.*

12. Setting words to music

EXAMPLE 37   'Let's go home and have some tea'.
Example 37 is a line from a song. If you want to put this line to music as part of a song you first have to decide which words are important, because these are the ones that you will want to be accented when sung.

Exercise 37a   *Try saying the line with accents on the underlined words:*
Let's go home and have some tea.

Exercise 37b   *Now try it this way:*
Let's go home and have some tea.
Most people would agree that the way suggested in exercise 37a sounds right, whilst 37b sounds rather silly.

One reason for this is that the second way (37b) accents words which are not important to the meaning of the sentence. You might imagine getting a phone message in which the line was so bad you could only hear half of the words. If you heard the accented words from 37a ('Lets home have tea') you would probably understand the message. On the other hand if you only heard the words accented in 37b ('go and some') it would be hard to know what it was all about. Clearly the words accented in 37a are more important than those accented in 37b.

EXAMPLE 38

There is a very clear relationship between accented words in music and where they come in a bar of music.

The first note after a bar line is heavily accented, and so the word sung on that note needs to be an important word. In a bar of $\frac{4}{4}$ the note that starts the second half of the bar is also accented. This will be the note equal to the third crotchet beat in a bar.

After that in importance come the notes on the second and fourth crotchet beats.

22

If the crotchets are divided into quavers, the second of each pair of quaver beats are the least important and least accented notes of all.

Exercise 38   Mark in the two most accented notes in this bar of music.

EXAMPLE 39

Let's go home and have some tea

If we imagine that this line is equal to one bar of music we can see first of all that it will have four accents in the bar. These could be the four main accents that can be found in one bar of $\frac{4}{4}$. Each accented word could be the start of each crotchet beat. However, that would leave the three unaccented words without any notes at all. So either we need more notes or more bars of music. Example 39 shows the solution using more notes. Where each accented word is followed by an unaccented word, the beat is divided into two quavers – the accented word of course being the first of each pair, as the first one holds the greater accent. The final result is shown in example 39.

That line from a song was quite easy to work out, but there is one complication that does arise. Some words have two syllables or more. Think of the word 'football'. It has two syllables 'foot' and 'ball'. Now think of the word 'Wenceslas' from the carol 'Good King Wenceslas looked out'. That word has three syllables: 'Wen-ces-las'.

Exercise 39a   *Work out a rhythm in $\frac{4}{4}$ for the line 'Good King Wenceslas looked out'. Write it down with the words underneath. You should find that it fits neatly into two bars, and all the notes are the same value, except the last one (for the 'out') which is a minim.*

Exercise 39b   *Now work out and write down the second line of the carol:*
'On the feast of Stephen'.
This line also has two bars, and the second bar has just one word in it: 'Stephen'. That word has two syllables, and each one should be given a minim.

EXAMPLE 40

Three blind mice,   Three blind mice,   See   how they run,   See how they run

Example 40 shows the first four lines of 'Three blind mice' written out in the rhythm that is normally used in this tune. Of course, other rhythms could be used, and they would be just as acceptable, as long as accented words fell on accented beats. For example, it would probably sound silly to accent the third line as '*see* how *they* run'. So to avoid accenting the word 'they', that word is put as the second of a pair of quavers; the least accented note possible.

Exercise 40a   *Write out the rhythm for the line 'Old Macdonald had a farm'.*
It fits into two bars of $\frac{4}{4}$. Put the words under the notes.

23

Exercise 40b   Write out a rhythm to these four lines from a pop song. Each line is one bar in $\frac{4}{4}$.

> Oh my baby,
> Don't you know,
> Oh my baby,
> I must go.

EXAMPLE 41   I don't know your name,
I only saw you yesterday.

Exercise 41   *Look at the first line shown in example 41. Decide what notes are going to be accented and write out a rhythm for the first line only.*

Many people will say that every word in the first line of example 41 is important, and so they would make each word a crotchet beat and see what happens. That works very well until we want to move on to the second line. The word 'name' ends the first line and there is a comma, so it would seem reasonable to pause there briefly before going on to the next line.

EXAMPLE 42

The problem is, how long should we pause on the word 'name'? Example 42a shows what happens if we just have two beats on that word. That means that the next bar starts with the second half of 'only', and no one would argue that 'ly' was the most important part of the next bar. Example 42b seems to be much better. It takes up three beats on 'name' (a dotted minim) and so starts the next bar with the first part of 'only'.

Exercise 42   *Write out the rhythm you would use to set example 41 to music.*
Use example 42b for the first three bars and put in the fourth bar yourself.

EXAMPLE 43   Old Macdonald had a farm,
E I E I O.
And on that farm he had a cow,
E I E I O.

Exercise 43   *Work out a rhythm to fit the words given in example 43.*
The first line has already been used in exercise 40a.
Here are a few points to help you:
a) Each line of the song takes up two bars.
b) The letter 'O' at the end of the second line takes a dotted minim. The fourth beat of that bar comes from the word 'and' at the start of the next line.
c) The very last bar will only have three crotchet beats in it, as the fourth beat will come from the next line of the song that is not shown here.

24

EXAMPLE 44   'Please take me home to my friends and my family'.

Exercise 44   *Work out the rhythm to the line from a song given in example 44. This is the first song you have met in this section that fits into $\frac{3}{4}$ time – with three crotchet beats to each bar.*
    Here are two hints:
a) There are four bars in all.
b) The word 'family' at the end can be said to have two syllables (fam-ily) or three (fa-mi-ly). It is probably best here to give it three syllables.

EXAMPLE 45   God save our gracious Queen,
        Long live our noble Queen,
        God save our Queen.

Exercise 45   *Work out the rhythm to these first three lines from the National Anthem.*
    Write it down with the words underneath.
    The piece is in $\frac{3}{4}$ time with a total of six bars. In bar 2 (for the words 'Gracious Queen') the rhythm is a dotted crotchet followed by a quaver and then a crotchet. The same pattern comes again for the end of line 2 in bar 4. The very last note is a dotted minim.

EXAMPLE 46

Exercise 46   *Look at the rhythm in example 46. Try and fit some words to it. It doesn't matter what the words are about, and they don't have to be good poetry. The main thing is to make the words fit.*

EXAMPLE 47

Exercise 47a   *As with exercise 46, try again to write some words for this rhythm.*

Exercise 47b   *Now try and write your own rhythm and your own words.*
    Be careful not to think up words that have a very difficult rhythm to them. It might be better to look back at some of the four-bar melodies you have written, and use their rhythms first of all before trying something more complicated.
    After you have practised doing this a few times, try and write a set of words and the musical rhythm for them that comes to eight bars, but don't try and write the melody for eight bars just yet.

13. Melody, rhythm and words

EXAMPLE 48

Take me back to   Eng - land, that's   where I   want to   be.

25

Exercise 48a   *Example 48 shows a four-bar song with words set to it. Write a four-bar song yourself and fit your own words to it. The process you should follow at this stage is:*
i) Write the four-bar tune according to the rules given before.
ii) Fit some words to this tune.
iii) If the words don't fit exactly, change the rhythm of the tune, or the words, until you get a perfect fit.

Exercise 48b   *Write another tune with words but this time work in a different order:*
i) Write the rhythm to a four-bar tune, only.
ii) Add the words to the rhythm.
iii) Write a melody to fit this set of rhythm and words.

Exercise 48c   *Write a third song with words, working in the following order:*
i) Write the words that you wish to use.
ii) Work out the rhythm to the words, so that they fit into four bars. If the words don't fit into four bars, change them so that they will. This does not mean that all songs have to fit into four bars, but it is, for the moment, simpler to stick to the rules you have been given.
iii) Work out a melody for the completed rhythm and words.

14. Passing notes

EXAMPLE 49

So far, all the songs that you have written have only used notes which are parts of chords. So, if you are writing a tune in the key of G major you might write it as in example 49. In the first bar you could use any of the notes available from the chords of G major – that is the notes G, B and D, and so on.

Exercise 49   *What chord would you take the notes from for the second bar of a song in G major? What would these notes be?*

EXAMPLE 50

Unfortunately the result of writing tunes in this way can be a little jumpy. The tunes you can write never run smoothly. In order to get this smooth effect it is necessary to use the notes between the notes of a chord. These are called PASSING NOTES. Example 50 shows a tune with passing notes used – they are all marked with an 'x'.

Exercise 50   *Complete the following table which relates to example 50.*
Key ......
Bar one is based on the chord of ......

26

The notes of the chord used in bar one are ......
The following note is also used, as a passing note in bar two ......
Bar two is based on the chord of ......
The notes of the chord used in bar two are ......
The following notes are also used, as passing notes in bar three ......

EXAMPLE 51

A passing note is a note between two other notes that fit into the chord that is being used as the basis for a bar. So if you are using the notes of the chord G for the first bar of your melody you have the notes G B and D. Between G and B there is one note in the scale of G major – the note A. A can be used as a passing note between G and B.

Exercise 51   *Look at example 51. Using crotchets only, fill in the missing notes – all of them will be passing notes.*

EXAMPLE 52

Example 52 is a four-bar tune in D major. Bars 1 and 3 include some passing notes – they are marked with an 'x'.

Exercise 52   *Copy out example 51, but rewrite bar 2 so that it includes one or two passing notes.*

EXAMPLE 53

Exercise 53   *Example 53 includes some passing notes. Which are they?*

EXAMPLE 54

Exercise 54a   *Example 54 includes some passing notes. Which are they?*

Exercise 54 b   *Write a four-bar tune that includes some passing notes.*

Exercise 54c   *Write a four-bar tune, including some passing notes, in key of D major, with a time signature of ¾.*

Exercise 54d   *Write a four-bar song, including words, using some passing notes.*

DON'T FORGET TO PLAY ALL THE EXAMPLES AND EXERCISES

27

15. The key of F major

EXAMPLE 55

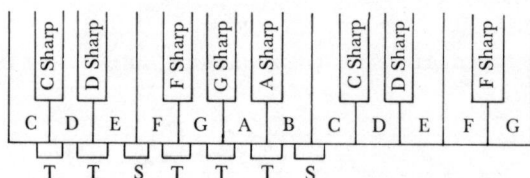

Example 55 shows the piano keyboard. You can work out the notes of any major scale by knowing which note it starts on, and remembering the fact that the distance between the notes of the scale (when going up the scale) should be:

Between the first and second note   tone (T)

Between the second and third note   tone (T)

Between the third and fourth note   semitone (ST)

Between the fourth and fifth note   tone (T)

Between the fifth and sixth note   tone (T)

Between the sixth and seventh note   tone (T)

Between the seventh and eight note   semitone (ST)

Don't forget that 1 tone = 2 semitones, and that a semitone is the distance between one note and the next note to it on the piano keyboard.

Exercise 55a   *What is the distance between F and G?*

What is the distance between G and A?

What is the distance between A and B?

What is the distance between E and F?

Exercise 55b   *If the first note of the scale of F major is F, what is*

   i) the second note?

   ii) the third note?

EXAMPLE 56

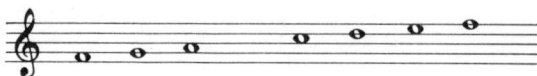

Example 56 shows the scale of F major with the fourth note missing. In answer to exercise 55b you should have found that the third note of the F major scale was A.

To find the fourth note it is necessary to move up from A by one semitone. If you look at the piano keyboard given in example 55 you'll see that the note one semitone above A is A sharp. If we were to write A sharp as the fourth note of the scale a problem would arise – sometimes we would want an 'A' and sometimes an 'A sharp'. How would we know which was which? How could we write a key signature of A sharp, when sometimes the A would not be sharp (when we wanted the third note of the scale)? There is another point. Look at the notes of the scales of C major, D major and G major:

C major: C D E F G A B C

D major: D E F shapr G A B C sharp D

G major: G A B C D E F sharp G

28

You'll see that every letter of the alphabet between A and G is used in each scale.

Exercise 56   *Look at the scale in example 56. Which letter of the alphabet between A and G is not used in that scale as a note?*

EXAMPLE 57

Example 57 should give you a clue as to how to get out of this problem. Just as a sharp raises any note by one semitone, it is possible to use a sign which lowers a note by one semitone. That sign is a FLAT. The names of the black notes can be given as either flats or sharps. In example 57 they are shown as flats and the notes they represent drawn underneath.

Exercise 57   *Draw the scale of F major, with B flat as the fourth note.*

EXAMPLE 58

Example 58 shows the key signature of F major. As the scale of F major contains no sharps and one flat (B flat) the key signature of F major contains one flat.

Exercise 58a   *Draw the key signatures of the following keys:*
   i) D major
   ii) C major
   iii) F major
   iv) G major.

Exercise 58b   As you know, the note A sharp can also be called B flat – and it is called B flat when used in the key of F major.
   Give the alternative names to the following notes:
   i) C sharp
   ii) D sharp
   iii) F sharp
   iv) G sharp.

EXAMPLE 59

Chord of F major   Chord of B flat major

Example 59 shows the chord of F major, followed by the chord of B flat major. If you are writing in the key of F major you will need to use those two chords as the basis for your notes in the first two bars of a four-bar tune.

Exercise 59   *Draw the chord of B flat major, followed by a chord of C major, and a chord of F major.*

29

EXAMPLE 60

The pattern of chords for a four-bar tune in F major is as follows:

Bar 1: F major
Bar 2: B flat major
Bar 3: C major
Bar 4: The note F.

This is the pattern of chords used in example 60. You will see that when a B flat is used in the tune the flat sign is not written in, as the B flat is in the key signature. You will also see that some passing notes are used.

Exercise 60   *Write a four-bar tune, without words, in F major.*

EXAMPLE 61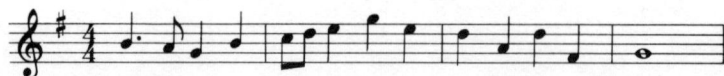

Example 61 shows the tune in example 60 transposed into G major. This means that every note is raised by one tone.

Exercise 61   *Transpose the tune written in answer to exercise 60 into G major.*

16. Eight-bar tunes

EXAMPLE 62

Example 62 shows a tune in the key of F major, consisting of eight bars, rather than the four you have used so far. There are two important points to note about writing eight-bar tunes. First, it is a good idea to have a resting point half way through the song (that is, in bar 4). A resting point is a bar or part of a bar where the notes are longer than in most of the rest of the tune. Here two minims are used. It is also possible to use a dotted minim and a crotchet.

As with so many rules in music, you will often find it broken in eight-bar tunes, but it is a good idea to stick to this rule at the moment. Having a resting point half way through a piece will give the tune more shape – the listener will hear it as four bars plus four bars, which is easier to take in than eight bars that have no resting point.

Second, the chord sequence. Here the chord sequence is F major; B flat major; F major; C major; F major; B flat major; C major; F major.

Each chord is used as the basis for one bar. Other sequences are possible – but for the exercise use this sequence.

Exercise 62   *Write an eight-bar tune in F major, in ⁴⁄₄ time, using the chord sequence given above, as the basis for the tune.*

30

EXAMPLE 63

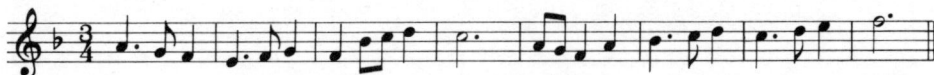

Example 63 is another eight-bar tune in F major. This time the chord sequence is: F major; C major; B flat major; F major; F major; B flat major; C major; F major.

As you know, it is possible to transpose a tune from one key into another. So it is also possible to transpose the chord sequence given as the basis for this tune into another key. In the exercise below you will find this chord sequence has already been transposed into G major.

Exercise 63   Complete the following table.

KEY	CHORD SEQUENCE 1 (example 62)	CHORD SEQUENCE 2 (example 63)
C major	....	....
G major	G major, C major, G major, D major G major, C major, D major, G major	....
D major	....	....
F major	F major, B♭ major, F major, C major F major, B♭ major, C major, F major	F major, C major, B♭ major, F major, F major, B♭ major, C major, F major

EXAMPLE 64

This example shows an eight-bar tune in C major.

Exercise 64a   Transpose the tune in example 64 into D major. Write out the chord sequence that is the basis of the tune under each bar.

Exercise 64b   Where is the resting point in example 64? What notes are used to make it a resting point?

EXAMPLE 65

Example 65 shows an eight-bar tune in D major.

Exercise 65   What is the chord sequence of the tune in example 65?

EXAMPLE 66   Example 66 summarizes the chord sequences used so far.
Example 62: Key F major.
Chord sequence: F major, B♭ major, F major, C major, F major, B♭ major, C major, F major
Example 63: Key F major.
Chord sequence: F major, C major, B♭ major, F major, F major, B♭ major, C major, F major

31

Example 64: Key C major
Chord sequence: C major, F major, G major, C major, C major, F major, G major, C major
Example 65: Key D major.
Chord sequence: D major, A major, G major, A major, G major, D major, A major, D major

Exercise 66 *Complete the chart given below so that each of the chord sequences is written out in each of the four keys used in this book. Set out the chart as follows.*

KEY	CHORD SEQ. 1 (example 61)	CHORD SEQ. 2 (example 62)	CHORD SEQ. 3 (example 63)	CHORD SEQ. 4 (example 64)
C major				
D major				
F major				
G major				

EXAMPLE 67

Exercise 67a *Answer the following questions about example 67.*
  i) What key is the piece in?
  ii) What is the time signature?
  iii) Where is the resting point?
  iv) What chord sequence is used?

Exercise 67b *Write an eight-bar tune in D major. Use a chord sequence given in exercise 66, and include a resting point in bar 4.*

Exercise 67c *Write an eight-bar song in G major, and fit some words to it. You can either start with the words, the rhythm or the melody.*

EXAMPLE 68

This example shows the first four bars of an eight-bar tune. From what is given it is possible to complete the tune. Obviously it is necessary to write in the same key, and to use the same sort of notes as used in the opening bars. The tune moves smoothly in crotchets and quavers up to the resting point – your answering tune should do the same. Use a chord sequence that follows on from the one given when completing the tune.

Exercise 68 *Complete the tune begun in example 68.*

EXAMPLE 69

Example 69 contains only the first two bars of an eight-bar tune. When completing

32

this, it will be rather like writing your own tune, except that you must stay in the same style as the music starts in.

Exercise 69   *Complete the tune started in example 69.*

EXAMPLE 70

Example 70 shows one possible way of completing example 69 – it will of course be different from the answer you gave. It shows how it is possible to use the information given in just two bars when building up a song. You will see that certain shapes and patterns (marked **a** and **b**) reappear in the later part of the song.

Exercise 70a   *Complete the following tune, re-using the opening phrase where appropriate.*

Exercise 70b   *Complete the following tune.*

EXAMPLE 71

Sometimes you may find a tune which you have to complete which does not seem to begin with a chord sequence you recognize. Example 71 is a case like this. Don't worry about that – just find an appropriate chord sequence from those you know.

Exercise 71   *Complete the tune started in example 71.*

17. Lower notes: the bass clef

EXAMPLE 72

F   G   A   B   C   D   E   F   G   A   B   C

So far, everything you have written has been in the treble clef. This means that most of the notes you have written have been fairly high notes. To write lower notes in the treble clef you had to draw in extra lines (leger lines) under the five lines given on the manuscript paper. Obviously, if you wanted to write very low notes the number of leger lines you would have to draw would be very large indeed. In order to be able to write lower notes without leger lines a different clef can be used on the stave – the BASS CLEF. This is shown in example 72.

Exercise 72   *Write the following words as notes using the bass clef:*
a) CABBAGE b) BADGE c) FACE d) BAGGAGE e) EGG.

33

EXAMPLE 73

It is important to know how the treble clef and bass clef overlap. In fact they meet, as shown in example 73, at MIDDLE C. This is the first note with a leger line through the middle of it below the last line in the treble clef, and above the top line in the bass clef. Whichever way it is drawn middle C is the same note – it is the C near the centre of the full piano keyboard.

Exercise 73   *Draw a bass clef, and then draw in all the notes from low F to middle C, as crotchets. Then draw a treble clef and continue upwards as crotchets to high G, without using middle C twice.*

EXAMPLE 74

Everything that has been demonstrated as being possible in the treble clef in this book is also possible in the bass clef. For example, it is quite possible to write four and eight-bar tunes in the bass clef. In fact, if you wrote the songs in the bass clef you would actually be writing the notes that men would sing, as the range of a man's voice is roughly the same as the range of notes available in the bass clef (without using leger lines). Of course this is not always true, as each man has a different range, some finding it harder than others to sing particularly high, or particularly low, notes.

Just as the bass clef covers the range of men's voices (BASSES and BARITONES), so the treble clef covers the range of most women's voices (ALTOS and SOPRANOS). If you wish to write a tune in the bass clef, you will need to know the key signatures used. Example 74 shows them.

Exercise 74   *Draw the key signature of a) G major, b) D major and c) F major first in the treble clef and then in the bass clef.*

EXAMPLE 75

Example 75 shows an eight-bar tune in the bass clef in G major.

Exercise 75   *Write an eight-bar tune, without words, in $\frac{4}{4}$ time, in the key of F major, in the bass clef.*

EXAMPLE 76

Example 76 gives the first two bars of a tune.

Exercise 76   *Complete the tune started in example 76, to make an eight-bar tune.*

EXAMPLE 77

Accompaniments to tunes generally use the bass clef a great deal. In example 77 a very simple accompaniment is put in. If you look at the treble clef you will see a simple tune in C major. The semibreves in the bass clef underneath are written to be played at the same time. Each one is the bottom note of the chord in each bar.

So, bar 1 is based on the chord of C major, and the bottom note of that chord (that is, the one it takes its name from – C) is put in the bass. In bar 2 the chord is, of course, F major and the chord's bottom note is therefore F. In bar 3 the chord is G major, and the note used in the bass is G. In the last bar, both parts end on C.

Exercise 77   *Write a bass part to the following tune. Copy out the tune and write the bass part underneath as shown in example 77.*

EXAMPLE 78A

Example 78a shows again how a bass accompaniment can be used, with just semibreves in the bass. This time it is in the key of D major. The three chords always used in the examples in this book when writing a four-bar tune in D major were D major, G major and A major (in that order). So in bar 1 the bass note is D, in bar 2 the bass note is G and in bar 3 the bass note is A. However, there is a problem at the point marked 'a'. Bar 2 ends with G in the bass and D in the treble. The distance between them is called a 'fifth' – that is there are five notes between G and D, counting G as 1 and D as 5.

Bar 3 also starts with a fifth – an E in the treble and an A in the bass. As both treble and bass have moved up one step the result is bound to be another fifth.

When two fifths come next to each other in this way the pattern is called 'consecutive fifths' and this is generally thought to sound bad: it should be avoided at all times. For the same reason, you should also avoid 'consecutive octaves', when the bass and treble part both play, for example, a G, and then immediately both play an A.

Example 78b shows example 78a re-written but with the consecutive fifths eliminated. They have now been replaced by the equally bad consecutive octaves!

EXAMPLES 78B AND 78C

Example 78c shows another version of example 78a, and this time both consecutive octaves and consecutive fifths have been removed.

Exercise 78a   *Without writing the whole piece, draw the consecutive fifths in example 78a.*

Exercise 78b   *Again without writing the whole piece, draw the consecutive octaves that appeared in example 78b.*

Exercise 78c   *Write a four-bar tune in D major, using both treble and bass clefs. Put the tune in the treble clef and an accompaniment of semibreves in the bass. Be careful to avoid consecutive fifths and octaves.*

EXAMPLE 79

Of course, if the bass accompaniment can only be in semibreves it will not be very exciting. Example 79 shows an accompaniment which uses minims as well.

The rules are similar to those for semibreves. First, think which chord is used as the basis for the bar. When writing a bass part with semibreves you could only use the bottom note of the chord (that is, the note from which the chord takes its name). Now you can use either the bottom note or the next note up in the chord.

However, there is one extra rule here. If this second note of the chord is used in the tune at the same moment as the bass note is to be played, do not put the same note in the bass as in the tune. Likewise, if the tune has the bottom note of the chord, put the next note (i.e., the middle note of the chord) in the bass.

Let's see how this works in example 79.

In bar 1 the chord used is C major. This means the bass can use either the bottom note (C) or the middle note (E) of this chord. In the first half of bar 1 an E appears in the treble clef, so the bass has a C. In the second half of bar 1 the treble clef has a C but no E, so that bass takes an E.

In bar 2 the chord used is F major. This means the bass can use either the bottom note (F) or the middle note (A). In the first half of bar 2 the treble clef has an F but no A, so the bass has an A. In the second half of bar 2 the situation is reversed.

In bar 3 the chord used is G major. This means the bass can use either the bottom note (G) or the middle note (B), of this chord. In the first half of the bar there is a B in the treble clef, so the bass takes a G. In the second half of the bar there is a G but no B in the treble clef, so the bass clef takes a B.

In bar 4 both parts end on the C.

Exercise 79a   *Write an accompaniment of minims to this four-bar tune in C major.*

Exercise 79b   *Write an accompaniment of minims to this four-bar tune in G major. The chord sequence is, of course, the same as for all four-bar tunes in G major used in this book – G major, C major, D major.*

36

Exercise 79c   Write an accompaniment of minims to this four-bar tune in D major.

Exercise 79d   Write an accompaniment of minims to this four-bar tune.

EXAMPLE 80

Example 80 shows an interesting problem – in each bar of the treble part both the bottom note and the middle note of the chord are used. When both notes are used what should be put in the bass? The answer is the bottom note of the chord. Always try to avoid doubling the middle note of a chord.

Exercise 80   Write a bass accompaniment to example 80. To save repeating the bass notes the minims can jump up or down an octave in each bar. When moving from one bar to the next, try to make the bass note move down if the treble moves upwards (as from bars 1 to 2). If the treble moves down (bars 2 to 3) the bass can move up. This makes the music sound more interesting.

EXAMPLE 81

Example 81 takes the bass accompaniment one stage further. It shows another interesting problem, for here the treble part contains minims itself. What should the bass do then? If it too contains minims the whole piece of music seems to get very slow indeed – or even come to a halt. This would be all right as a resting point half way through an eight-bar tune, but not in a short four-bar tune.

The answer, as you can see from example 81, is for the bass to include some extra movement. But it still obeys all the rules you have already learned about how to write a bass accompaniment but some use of the top note of the chord in the bass is now allowed. Study example 81 to see what the bass does before doing exercise 81 below.

Exercise 81a   Write an accompaniment to this treble part.

Exercise 81b   Write a bass accompaniment to this four-bar tune.

Exercise 81c   *Write a bass accompaniment to this four-bar tune.*

18. Another time signature: $\frac{6}{8}$

EXAMPLE 82

Example 82 shows a four-bar tune in G major, with the time signature of $\frac{6}{8}$. The number 6 at the top of the time signature means 6 beats in a bar, whilst the number 8 at the bottom means the beats are quavers. So $\frac{6}{8}$ means six quavers in a bar. In $\frac{6}{8}$ time it is important to bear in mind that each bar is divided into two equal parts, so that quavers are grouped in threes.

Exercise 82   *a) What does $\frac{6}{8}$ mean, when written as a time signature?*
               b) How are quavers usually grouped in $\frac{6}{8}$ time?

EXAMPLE 83

Example 83 shows some of the various ways possible of writing bars in $\frac{6}{8}$ time. Only the very last one (the dotted minim) breaks the rule about showing two groups of the equivalent of three quavers. The dotted lines show where the middle of the bar is. It is important always to be able to see where this middle is, in bars of $\frac{6}{8}$. The single dotted minim is, of course, the exception.

Exercise 83   *Write the rhythm you would use, if writing a four-bar tune in $\frac{6}{8}$ time.*

EXAMPLE 84

Example 84 shows another tune in $\frac{6}{8}$ time.

Exercise 84a   *Write a four-bar tune in the key of C major in $\frac{6}{8}$ time. Remember to use only the rhythms shown in example 83, so that you will always show the middle of each bar.*

Exercise 84b   *Write a four-bar tune in D major in $\frac{6}{8}$ time.*

EXAMPLE 85

Example 85 shows a song in ⁶⁄₈ time with an accompaniment. This is just a combination of the rules you learned about writing music in two parts, and the rules about writing in ⁶⁄₈ time.

Exercise 85a   Write an accompaniment to the following piece.

Exercise 85b   Complete the following opening to make a four-bar tune.

EXAMPLE 86

Example 86 shows another tune in ⁶⁄₈ time.

Exercise 86   Write some words to fit to the tune given in example 86.

EXAMPLE 87

Example 87 shows an eight-bar tune in ⁶⁄₈. All the rules of writing in ⁶⁄₈ still apply.

Exercise 87a   Write an eight-bar tune in ⁶⁄₈ time, in C major.

Exercise 87b   Write an eight-bar tune in ⁶⁄₈ time, in F major.

19. Rests

EXAMPLE 88   NOTES

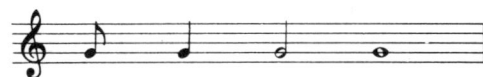

RESTS

Quaver   Crotchet   Minim   Semibreve

A crotchet rest can also be written 𝄽.

So far, in all the music you have written, there has never been an occasion when silence was required. However, sometimes it is very necessary to have silence – for example, in a piece of music composed for a large number of instruments. It is not often that the composer would want all the instruments to play all the time.

Therefore a sign is needed to show when the instrument or singer concerned should not play or sing. When this is required RESTS are written into the music.

39

The length of a rest can vary, just as the length of a note can. So there are various types of rest – a quaver rest, a crotchet rest, a minim rest and a semibreve rest. They are shown in example 88. All rests last as long as a note of that value.

Exercise 88   *Draw a quaver, minim, crotchet and semibreve, and next to each note put a rest of the same value. Remember that a minim rest always sits on the third line of the stave, while the semibreve rest hangs from the fourth line.*

20. Notes (continued) semiquavers

EXAMPLE 89

SEMIQUAVERS (or 16th-notes) are half as long as quavers. Example 89 shows one semiquaver, followed by a group of semiquavers. At the end is a semiquaver rest.

Exercise 89   *Complete the following chart.*

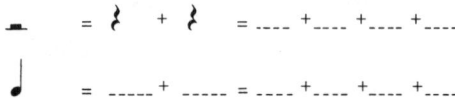

EXAMPLE 90

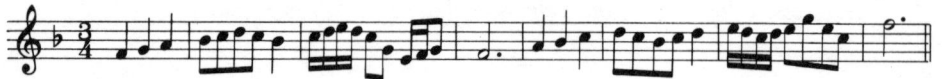

This example shows an eight-bar tune in which semiquavers are used. Notice that very short notes like semiquavers are not normally used next to long notes like minims, as this tends to make the music very jumpy.

Exercise 90   *Write an eight-bar tune in F major using a number of semiquavers.*

21. More major keys and scales

EXAMPLE 91

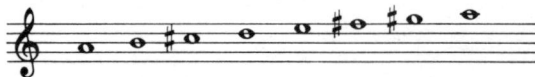

Scale of A major

Example 91 shows the scale of A major. Like all major scales it follows that same pattern of distances between each pair of notes: Tone, tone, semitone, tone, tone, tone, semitone.

Thus the distance between the first note and the second is a tone, between the second and third is a tone, the third and fourth is a semitone, and so on.

Exercise 91   *Write the scale of A major in the bass clef.*

40

EXAMPLE 92

Example 92 shows the key signature of A major in the treble and bass clefs.

Exercise 92   *Draw a bass clef, then put the key signature of A major, and then draw a scale of A major starting with the highest note and coming down to the bottom. Remember you do not have to put in the sharps next to the notes, as they are given in the key signature.*

EXAMPLE 93
Scale of E major

Example 93 shows the scale of E MAJOR with key signature, in the treble clef.

Exercise 93   *Draw the scale of E major in the bass clef, without key signature.*

EXAMPLE 94

Example 94 shows the key signature of E major in the bass clef.

Exercise 94   *Draw the key signatures of the following keys, first in the treble clef, and then in the bass clef:*
C major; G major; D major; A major; E major.

EXAMPLE 95
Chord of E major   Chord of B major

If you wish to write any tunes in the keys of A major or E major you will need to use one or two chords not met before in this book, as the basis for the melody. Example 95 shows the chords of E major and B major. If you wish to write in the key of A major the three chords you will need for a four-bar tune are:
    Bar 1 – A major; Bar 2 – D major; Bar 3 – E major; Bar 4 – note A. For the key of E major you will need the following chords:
    Bar 1 – E major; Bar 2 – A major; Bar 3 – B major; Bar 4 – note E.

Exercise 95a   *Write a four-bar tune in A major.*

Exercise 95b   *Write a four-bar tune in E major.*
Note: Remember that you must put the key signature before each of these songs, and that having done that there is no need to put any sharps in the piece of music you are writing.

EXAMPLE 96
B flat major   E flat major   A flat major

Example 96 shows the key signature of three keys – each of which adds one more flat to the key signature of the previous key. You have already been introduced to the key of F major, which has one flat.

41

Exercise 96   Draw the scales (treble and bass) of F major, B flat major, E flat major and A flat major. Put the correct key signature before each scale. This will mean you do not need to draw in the flats next to the notes of the scales.

EXAMPLE 97

Chord of E flat major   Chord of A flat major   Chord of D flat major

In the key of F major, the following chords were used when writing tunes: F major, B flat major, C major.

In the keys of B flat major, E flat major and A flat major use the chords shown in the chart below:

Key	Bar 1	Bar 2	Bar 3	Last note in tune
B flat major	B♮ major	E♭ Major	F major	B♭
E flat major	E♭ major	A♭ major	B♭ major	E♭
A flat major	A♭ major	D♭ major	E♭ major	A♭

Example 97 shows the chords of E flat major, A flat major and D flat major. All the other chords have been introduced before.

Exercise 97a   Write a four-bar tune in B flat major, with a simple accompaniment of semibreves in the bass.

Exercise 97b   Write an eight-bar tune in ⁶₈ time in A flat major.

Exercise 97c   Write an eight-bar tune in ¾ time in E flat major.

22. The natural

EXAMPLE 98

Example 98 shows the notes B flat, B natural, D sharp and D natural. The idea of the NATURAL is to cancel out a sharp or a flat.

If, in a piece of music a note should be played as a sharp, because that is in the key signature, and the composer wants to remove the sharp, he will write in a natural before the note concerned. The same applies to a flat – the natural before a note that should be a flat cancels out the flat.

Exercise 98   Draw the following notes in the bass clef – C sharp, C natural, B flat, B natural.

EXAMPLE 99

It is important to realize that the note D natural is exactly the same note as you have always previously called D. It is only called D natural to emphasize that it is not D sharp or D flat.

In example 99 you can see that a natural is repeated in each bar. A natural only lasts until the next bar line. If the note G is changed from G sharp to G natural, all the Gs for the rest of the bar are changed to G natural as well. However, the bar line cancels out the natural, and if the composer wants the note to remain G natural he has to write in another natural sign in the next bar before the G.

Exercise 99   *Change this piece of music, so that all the F sharps are turned into F naturals. Do not put in more natural signs than are needed.*

23. Minor keys and scales

EXAMPLE 100   Scale of C major

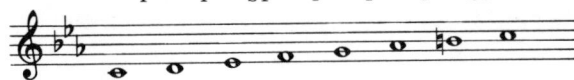

Scale of C minor

All the scales so far dealt with in this book are major scales. That means they have the following distances between the notes of the scale (see table above):

Between the first and second notes   tone (T)
Between the second and third notes   tone (T)
Between the third and fourth notes   semitone (ST)
Between the fourth and fifth notes   tone (T)
Between the fifth and sixth notes   tone (T)
Between the sixth and seventh notes   tone (T)
Between the seventh and eighth notes   semitone (ST)

It doesn't matter which note you start on – you can build up a major scale using that table. In major scales the distances never vary.

In MINOR scales a different set of distances apply.
There are two types of minor scales – the HARMONIC and MELODIC. The melodic minor is the one generally used for melodies and songs, the harmonic minor for harmonies and chords. Example 100 shows the scales of C major and C (harmonic) minor.

Exercise 100   *Draw the scale of C minor, descending (that is, going from the top note to the bottom) using crotchet notes.*

43

EXAMPLE 101   Scale of C major

Scale of A minor

The harmonic minor scales have the following distances between the notes of the scale:

Between the first and second note   tone (T)
Between the second and third note   semitone (ST)
Between the third and fourth note   tone (T)
Between the fourth and fifth note   tone (T)
Between the fifth and sixth note   semitone (ST)
Between the sixth and seventh note   three semitones (one tone and one semitone) (3ST)
Between the seventh and eighth note   semitone (ST)

Example 101 shows the scales of C major and A harmonic minor. You may be surprised to find that the key of C minor has a key signature of three flats, whilst the key of C major has no sharps or flats in the key signature. Even more strange is the key signature of A minor, which is the same as C major. You'll find out why in a moment.

Exercise 101   *Draw a scale of A minor in the bass clef, and over the top of each pair of notes write the distance between them.*

EXAMPLE 102

Example 102 shows the key signatures of the minor scales up to four sharps and four flats. The minor scales take their key signatures from the 'relative major' scale – that is, the major scale that starts three semitones above the first note of the minor scale.

The relative major of A minor is C major. This means both A minor and C major have the same key signature.

The relative major of C minor is E flat major. This means both C minor and E flat major have the same key signature.

Exercise 102   *Work out the relative majors of: D minor, F minor, B minor, E minor, F sharp minor, C sharp minor, G minor.*

EXAMPLE 103

44

F sharp minor

C sharp minor

D minor

G minor

F minor

Just as it is possible to speak of relative majors, one can also speak of relative minors. The relative minor of a key is the minor scale that starts three semitones below the start of the major scale.

Example 103 shows various minor scales.

Exercise 103 *What are the relative major scales of the minor scales shown in example 103?*

EXAMPLE 104

Flats in key signature

		0	1	2	3	4
Sharps in key signature	0	C major A minor	F major D minor	B♭ major G minor	E♭ major C minor	A♭ major F minor
	1	G major E minor				
	2	D major B minor				
	3	A major F♯ minor				
	4	E major C♯ minor				

Example 104 shows the key signatures of all the keys up to four sharps and flats, giving both the major and minor scale that uses the key signature shown.

Exercise 104 *Draw the key signature and scale of G major and its relative minor.*
Draw the key signature and scale of D minor and its relative major.

EXAMPLE 105

Scale of A harmonic minor

Scale of A melodic minor

45

Example 105 shows the scale of A HARMONIC MINOR, and below A MELODIC MINOR, both ascending and descending. You will see that the scale of A melodic minor changes on the way down. The descending form of the melodic minor *always* changes on the way down. The descending form of the melodic minor exactly represents the key signature. The naturals shown here exactly cancel out the sharps added on the way up, leaving no sharps at all – which is the key signature of A minor.

The harmonic and melodic minor scales of the same key take exactly the same key signature. Thus the key signature of C harmonic minor is the same as C melodic minor. (These are of course both the same as the key signature of E flat major – the relative major.) The distances between the notes of a melodic minor scale are as follows:

Ascending

    Between the first and second note   tone (T)
    Between the second and third note   semitone (ST)
    Between the third and fourth note   tone (T)
    Between the fourth and fifth note   tone (T)
    Between the fifth and sixth note   tone (T)
    Between the sixth and seventh note   tone (T)
    Between the seventh and eighth note   semitone (ST)

Descending

    Between the eighth and seventh note   tone (T)
    Between the seventh and sixth note   tone (T)
    Between the sixth and fifth note   semitone (ST)
    Between the fifth and fourth note   tone (T)
    Between the fourth and third note   tone (T)
    Between the third and second note   semitone (ST)
    Between the second and first note   tone (T)

Exercise 105a   *Draw the following scales with key signature, ascending and descending, in melodic minor form:*
A minor, E minor, B minor.

In order to work out these scales, simply copy the harmonic minor scale but for the *ascending* form raise the sixth note by one semitone. For the *descending* form just make sure the scale includes the sharps or flats given in the key signature.

Exercise 105b   *Draw the following scales with key signatures, ascending and descending, in melodic minor form:*
F sharp minor, F minor, C minor.

Exercise 105c   *Draw the following scales with key signatures, ascending and descending, in melodic minor form:*
G minor, D minor.

DON'T FORGET TO PLAY ALL THE EXAMPLES AND EXERCISES

24. Some hints on writing melodies

EXAMPLE 106

Example 106 shows a tune (or melody) with two weak points in it. Although it breaks none of the rules given so far, many people would consider it a poor melody.

First, it contains a series of upward leaps (marked **a**). Generally speaking after two leaps in one direction it is better to bring the melody back again. Otherwise it sounds as if the tune is going in one direction forever.

The other problem usually comes at the end of the tune. In the last bar but one you will usually use the seventh note of the scale of the key you are in. Here the note is D♯ – the seventh note of the scale of E major. This seventh note (usually called the leading note) should move up one step in the next bar to the E, rather than fall down to the E below. So the rule is, where ever the leading note occurs in the last but one bar, take it up one step in the last bar, to give the final note.

Exercise 106   *Correct the weak points marked 'a' and 'b' in example 106, by writing out the complete tune, with changes made at these two points.*

EXAMPLE 107

This example introduces another point about writing tunes. Above the music you will see some curved lines called PHRASE MARKS. Phrase marks are rather like commas in writing – they help the person reading the piece to make more sense of it. At the end of a phrase there is a very short break, rather like the very slight pause a person will make when reading a sentence, at each comma. Normally the phrases are played smoothly, so that the little break at the end of a phrase is emphasized.

Exercise 107a   *Add phrase marks to this melody.*

EXAMPLE 108

Example 108 shows a tune in which, at a certain point, a note is repeated on either side of a bar line. Sometimes it makes an interesting effect if this note is not repeated, but held, as if the original note had been double the value. Of course, it is impossible to write that note at a longer value because the bar would then have too many beats in it. So the notes are written in the normal way but a little line is drawn between the two notes – as shown in the example, in bars 2 and 3. This is called a TIE – the second note of the pair is not played but is held.

47

Exercise 108a Copy out example 107 and exercise 107a. To example 107 add two ties (one joining notes in the different halves of the same bar).
To exercise 107a add one tie.

Exercise 108b Write an eight-bar tune which includes at least one tie.

EXAMPLE 109

I	II	III	IV	V	VI	VII	VIII
Tonic	Supertonic	Mediant	Sub Dominant	Dominant	Sub Mediant	Leading Note	I or Tonic

Example 109 shows the scale of E major, with the notes numbered. In example 109 it was pointed out that the seventh note of the scale can have a special name – the LEADING NOTE.

In fact all the notes of a scale have their own name, as follows.
First note – TONIC (I)
Second note – SUPERTONIC (II)
Third note – MEDIANT (III)
Fourth note – SUBDOMINANT (IV)
Fifth note – DOMINANT (V)
Sixth note – SUBMEDIANT (VI)
Seventh note – LEADING NOTE (VII)
Eighth note – TONIC (I)

Sometimes these notes are written as Roman numerals, as shown next to the names, although often the figures refer to the chords built up on these notes. So in the key of C major the subdominant is F, and the chord of F major (in the key of C major) could be written as IV.

Exercise 109 What are the following notes:
a) The subdominant of D major?
b) The leading note of E major?
c) The dominant of F major?
d) The tonic of G major?

EXAMPLE 110

It is perfectly possible to change keys part way through a tune. It is then possible to change back again to the original key. Normally the changes are to one of the following keys: the subdominant, the dominant, the relative major or the relative minor.

Any change of key in a piece is called a MODULATION.

It is easy to recognize a key change or modulation in a piece as it will be shown by the placing of one or more sharps, flats or naturals in the music.

The main question is, what key has the melody changed to?
Here are some hints:

If the fourth note of a scale is raised one semitone the modulation is to the dominant of the old key.

If the seventh note of a scale is lowered one semitone the modulation is to the subdominant of the old key.

If the tune is in a major key and the fifth note is raised by one semitone the modulation is to the relative minor.

When you think you have found the new key you can check by looking to see if the tonic of the new key is in the bars immediately after the modulation. There will probably be a move to the dominant chord of the new key immediately before the first bar in the new key.

In example 110 the modulation is from C major to G major. The fourth note of the scale of C major is raised one semitone (to F sharp), and in the next bar, the note G can be found.

Exercise 110   *What keys do the following tunes start in, and what do they modulate to?*
All the tunes return to their original keys by the end of the piece.

a

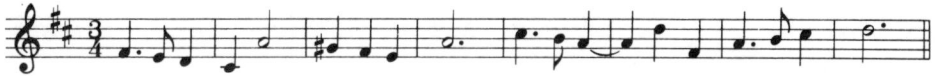

b

c

d

25. Cadences

A perfect cadence

EXAMPLE 111

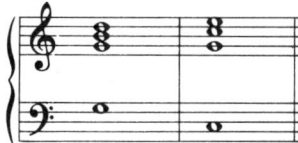

In writing a four-bar tune in C major, the following chord sequence was used as a basis for the tune: C major; F major; G major; C major.

In the last bar of course only the note C was used, implying the chord of C major.

If the chords were given numbers, based on the note of the scale of C major they were built up from, the sequence would read: I; IV; V; I.

All the tunes shown in this book that were four bars long were based on this sequence, whatever key they were in. Any tune that ends with this V–I sequence is said to end in a PERFECT CADENCE. Cadences are rather like 'punctuation marks' in writing; they are chord progressions which break up the music into phrases and sentences.

Note that it is not so much the notes that are important as the chord that the notes represent. In fact if you listen to the chords only, it is easier to hear the cadence – the chords are drawn in example 111 for a perfect cadence.

It is also possible to have other types of cadence.

A cadence moving from Chord IV to Chord I is a PLAGAL cadence.

A cadence moving from Chord IV to Chord V is an IMPERFECT cadence.

A cadence moving from Chord I to Chord V is also an imperfect cadence.

Exercise 111a   *Look at these pairs of chords, and state what sort of cadence is implied.*

Exercise 111b   *Look back to the four chord sequences given in exercise 66.*
Write out the four difference types of chord sequence using the Roman numerals, I, IV and V, with I representing the tonic chord, IV representing the subdominant chord and V representing the dominant chord.

Exercise 111c   *Look at the chord sequence for bars 3 and 4 of the eight-bar songs that you have worked out in exercise 110b. What cadences are used in the four different chord sequences at the half-way point in the eight-bar tunes?*

Conclusion

Now that you have reached the end of the theory section of this book you should have a basic understanding of the theory of musical notation. This theory should help you understand how a great deal of classical music, as well as some pop music, has been written.

Obviously there are many more things to learn in the theory of music, so you should not be surprised if, when you come to read certain pieces of music, you find that it includes some signs or symbols that you have not come across. Equally do not be surprised if you find that some of the rules given here have been broken. Just as there is often more than one accepted spelling of a word, it is possible to break nearly all these musical rules at some time. However, it is still necessary to know the rules first.

So that musicians can express themselves more fully they often give directions about the speed or style in which a piece should be played. By tradition these directions are usually written in Italian and these words and their meaning are given in section 4 of the book. Composers also use various special signs to indicate certain effects they require. Some of these special signs are given on the next page.

Musical signs and ornaments

Get louder. (Italian word: CRESCENDO)

Get softer. (Italian word: DIMINU-ENDO)

Play the notes under the line smoothly. (The curved line (called a SLUR) may be placed under the notes.) Don't confuse slurs with PHRASE MARKS (see page 47).

A TIE. The note is held, and not repeated.

Both signs mean accent that note: the first is a short, sharp accent; the second a heavier stress.

The note is to be played in a short, detached fashion. The Italian word is STACCATO.

Pause – found over or under a note or rest, usually at the end of a piece.

8va

Play an octave higher. If found under the music it means play an octave lower.

Repeat all the music between the dots. If only the sign at the end appears it means repeat from the start of the music.

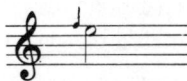

The little note is an APPOGGIATURA. It takes half the value of the note that follows it.

The little note with a line through it is an ACCIACCATURA. It is played as quickly as possible.

A TRILL. Play the note shown and the note immediately above it in the key of the piece one after the other as quickly as possible.

So this E might be played:

A TURN.

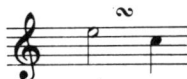

It is played as follows:

A MORDENT.

It is played as follows:

51

♩ =60′ indicates that the piece should be played at a speed which allows 60 crotchets beats to be played every minute. (This means of course one crotchet every second.) This is a reference to the METRONOME marking. A metronome is a mechanical instrument for fixing the speed at which a piece of music is to be played. It has a metal rod which swings backwards and forwards, engraved with numbers that correspond to the number of beats per minute.

♩ =120′ indicates 120 crotchets every minute or 2 crotchets per second. It is possible for any number and any note to give a speed indication.

Thus a ♩ =90′ sign means 90 minim beats every minute.

SECTION 2
The history of music

>Bach; Beethoven; Berlioz; Brahms; Britten; Chopin; Copland; Dvořák; Elgar; Handel; Haydn; Mendelssohn; Mozart; Purcell; Schubert; Schumann; Sibelius; Shostakovich; Stravinsky; Tchaikovsky; Vaughan Williams; Wagner.

Note to the teacher

At the end of each section of musical history can be found ten questions and some suggestions for listening. The answers to the questions can generally be found in the text, although sometimes it will be necessary for students to look up further information in the subsequent sections on important composers, instruments and musical words. Where a term is referred to in the section of definitions it is shown in the text in **bold** type.

The records chosen as suggested listening are given with their English catalogue numbers. Where high-class recordings are available at budget prices these have been chosen in preference to more expensive versions.

IOANNIS PETRI
Loysij Praeneftini in basilica
S. Petri de vrbe capellae
Magistri.
MISSARVM LIBER PRIMVS.

PARTHENIA
or
THE MAYDENHEAD
of the first musicke that
euer was printed for the VIRGINALLS.
COMPOSED
By three famous Masters: William Byrd. D: John Bull, & Orlando Gibbons
Gentilmen of his Ma:tis most illustrious Chappell.
Dedicated to all the Maisters and Louers of Musick.
Ingrauen
by William Hole.
for
Dorethie Euans.
Cum
Priuilegio.

Printed at LONDON by G. Lowe and are to be foulde
at his howse in Loathberry

The 16th century (1550–1620)

(top) *A Flemish painting of a family making music; the lady on the right is playing the virginals, the man in the centre the lute*

(bottom right) *Title page of the* Parthenia *printed in about 1611. This was the first collection of printed* music *for the virginals, and contained pieces by* William Byrd, John Bull, and Orlando Gibbons

(bottom left) *Palestrina presenting his book of masses to the Pope*

The period of musical history covered by this book starts in 1550. But of course there was music before this date. Men and women have made music, and listened to it, since the human race began. However, it is quite sensible to start a history of music at around 1550, as by then some composers were writing music that is still widely appreciated today, and is easily available on record. In recent years earlier music has also begun to be popular and more and more of it is being recorded.

In the second half of the 16th century, many educated people knew something about music. Ever since the 6th century B.C., the theory of music had been thought to be very important in man's understanding of the universe. At that time, it was well known that the note made by a plucked string depends on the length of the string, and that there is a very exact mathematical link between the change in the length of the string and the change in the pitch of the note. For example, if you halve the length of a string the pitch will go up by one octave. Relationships such as these were thought to be so important that they influenced many architects and planners in their designs. Music was thus seen as one of the most important of all the arts.

The music of the 16th and early 17th centuries is often recognizable for its use of the old system of **modes**, and is very *Polyphonic* **contrapuntal** in character. This may make it seem rather strange to anyone who is only used to hearing music written in later periods.

Most of the music composed at this time was vocal music – the main forms of religious music were the **mass** and the **motet**. Composers were engaged to write particular pieces of music for church services.

In secular (that is, non-religious) music, the main vocal form was the **madrigal** which was most often sung in the homes of the aristocracy. A particularly highly talented group of madrigal composers from England wrote some of the best madrigals ever composed, during the last 30 years of this period.

Instruments were often used in the home to play contrapuntal music – the most popular instruments being the **viols** and **recorders**. Many madrigals were re-written so that they could be played on viols instead of being sung. There were also many songs written for accompaniment by a **lute**.

One of the most important composers of sacred music in this period was Palestrina. He spent most of his life in Rome, and wrote over 100 masses and 250 motets. At the time some members of the Catholic Church wanted to ban harmonized vocal writing in two or more parts, because it made the words of the service more difficult to understand. The Council of Trent was the official body considering the matter, and it was because of the works of Palestrina and a number of other Italian composers that the Council decided that such music could be both beautiful and understandable, and deserved a place in the church.

In England, one of the best known composers was William Byrd. He wrote three unaccompanied masses to Latin words, as well as motets, madrigals and many keyboard compositons.

QUESTIONS

1. Why was music thought to be of particular importance in the 16th century?

2. What happens to a note made by a plucked string when the length of the string is doubled?

3. What art form did music particularly influence during this period?

4. What is a **mode**?

5. Name and describe two forms of vocal religious music from the period.

6. What is the meaning of 'secular' music?

7. What is a **madrigal**?

8. When did a great school of madrigal writing flourish in England?

9. What is a **viol**?

10. Name two major composers from this period and state what sort of music they wrote.

LISTENING

Palestrina *Missa Papae Marcelli* HMV HQS 1237

Byrd *Mass for three voices* Argo ZRG 5362

The early Baroque period (1620–1700)

The elaborately decorated organ in a 17th-century baroque church in Austria

The 17th century represents the first part of the Baroque era, which lasted until around 1750. The word 'baroque' comes from the architectural style of the time – highly decorated and ornamental buildings with many twists and curls.

In the Baroque era, composers were employed, as they had always been, by patrons – either the church or wealthy individuals who hired musicians to write and perform music on particular occasions. Lully, for example, wrote music for the court of King Louis XIV in France. The music was therefore composed to order, rather than being written when the composer felt inclined. This system of patronage, as it was called, was in operation until the early 19th century, when composers like Beethoven began to break free and follow their own musical inclinations.

There were, however, many new developments in the music of the early Baroque period. The old modal system of earlier times was rapidly becoming

57

(opposite) *Lully and his fellow musicians at the French court of Louis XIV*

outdated, and being replaced by the major and minor scales, which are familiar today.

In vocal music, there was a move away from the style of writing that had been fashionable earlier, in which the words sometimes became unintelligible due to the complicated musical arrangement. Composers tried much more to reflect the meaning of the words when setting them to music. This can be seen clearly in the most important new development of this period, the invention of **opera**, around the year 1600.

Opera first became fashionable in Italy, and later in France, Germany, and to a lesser extent England. The first operas were performed in the houses of the rich, but in 1637 the first public opera house was opened in Venice. This was so successful that many others followed.

Early operas consisted largely of **recitative**, with a few short **arias** and **choruses**. But the arias quickly became important, as audiences plainly showed that they really came to opera to hear well-known performers singing very expressive and ornate pieces. This was probably the origin of the idea of the 'star' performer.

The demands of opera caused many changes in musical composition during the 17th century. One new idea was the **basso continuo**. A bass line was written with chord symbols underneath it, from which the harpsichordist could read which chords were needed, and could improvise an accompaniment around them. The notion of the star performer, on the other hand, was reflected in the idea of the virtuoso – someone particularly good at singing or playing an instrument. Vivaldi wrote a number of works for solo violin which enabled virtuoso players to show off their talents.

The first great operatic composer was Monteverdi, whose works showed many new ways of using harmonies and chords. The idea of **harmonic progression** was to become more and more important as the century progressed. Monteverdi was also the first composer to use the effect of very rapidly repeated notes on the violin (called **tremolo**). He used a large number of instruments to accompany his operas: although they were very different from the instruments used in modern orchestras, Monteverdi's work is generally recognized as the foundation of the idea of the orchestra as we know it today.

Because of this interest in opera and the growing awareness of musical instruments, the instruments themselves began to develop and change. The older viols were gradually replaced by the instruments that make up the string section of the modern orchestra, the violin, viola, cello, and double bass, which were thought to be more flexible and versatile. Composers learned how to write effectively for different instruments, bringing out their special characteristics. Couperin, a French composer, wrote 27 harpsichord **suites** with dance-like movements in **binary** form, whilst the Italian composer Corelli wrote 60 **sonatas**, mostly for two violins, cello and harpsichord. The harpsichord played the **continuo** part, an idea which had been first developed in operatic writing.

One other composer who must be mentioned here was the Englishman Purcell, who was also a great organist. He started by composing sonatas similar to those of Corelli, and also wrote one opera – *Dido and Aeneas*. The fact that he only wrote

(top) *Antonio Vivaldi, Italian composer who wrote over 400 Concerti grossi*

(bottom) *Claudio Monteverdi, the first great Italian composer of operas*

59

A 17th-century gathering. Notice the young man conducting with a roll of paper

one opera shows that this form was of less interest to English audiences than to those in Europe. However, he did write the music for a number of plays including *The Fairy Queen*, which was an adaptation of Shakespeare's *Midsummer Night's Dream*. He also wrote much church music, including anthems and settings of the psalms.

QUESTIONS

1. Describe the change that took place in the writing of vocal music in this period.
2. Give and example of a musician who received patronage during the 17th century and name his patron. What did his patron do for him?
3. Name the instruments in the string section of the orchestra.
4. Describe a cello.
5. What is an opera?
6. In which countries did opera become fashionable in the 17th century?
7. Explain the meaning of **recitative** and **basso continuo**.
8. Write briefly about the music of Monteverdi.
9. Describe the suite of this period and name a composer who wrote suites.
10. Who was the main English composer of this period? Write a few lines about his music.

LISTENING

Lully *Pièces de symphonie* Oiseau Lyre SOL 301
Monteverdi *Orfeo* (highlights) Telefunken AN 641175
Couperin *Les Nations* Telefunken DX 648009
Corelli *Concerti grossi Opus 6* Argo ZRG 828
Purcell *Dido and Aeneas* Oiseau Lyre SOL 60047
  Fairy Queen Decca SET 499/500
  Fairy Queen (highlights) Decca SET 560
  Music for the Chapel Royal Argo ZRG 5444

CORELLI: *Concerto Grosso No. 8*

1. II = 2nd movement.

2. Allegro = fast.

3. Two flats = the key signature. Two flats can either mean D major or G minor. If the key is G minor we can expect to see some F sharps in the score, and there is in fact one in the first bar. The piece therefore is clearly in G minor.

4. C = the time signature. The C stands for common time, or $\frac{4}{4}$.

5. Concertino = the three soloists in concerti grossi. The top line is for a violin, the middle line for a second violin and the third line for a cello.

6. Ripieno = the main orchestra. Here the top line is the first violins, the second line for the second violins, the third line for the violas and the bottom line for the cellos.

7. The viola clef. On this clef middle C is on the middle line.

8. f = forte (loud).

9. $\frac{6}{5}$ These figures under the cello part, plus the occasional sharps are the 'figured bass' to be played by the harpsichord. The harpsichordist works out what the chords should be from reading the numbers and the bass line. Where no numbers are given it means the tonic chord should be played.

1550

1560

1570   Monteverdi 1567-1643 4 + 5

1580

1590

1600   Palestrina 1525-1594 8

1610

1620   10 12

William Byrd 1543-1623

1630   13 29
        Lully 1632-1687

1640

1650   Corelli 1653-1733 16
        Purcell 1659-1695 30
                            18
1660   A.Scarlatti 1660-1725

        Couperin 1668-1733 22
1670

1680   Vivaldi 1685-1741 25
        D.Scarlatti 1685-1757 26
                            27
        J.S.Bach 1685-1750
1690   Handel 1685-1759
                    28

1700

1558–1601 Reign of Elizabeth I

1564–1616 Shakespeare

1564–1642 Galileo

1577–80 Drake sails around the world

1588 Drake defeats Spanish Armada

1594 First opera performed: <u>Dafne</u> by Peri

1621 First English newspaper published

1637 First public opera house opened

1642 Civil War starts

1653 Cromwell becomes Lord Protector

1656 First English opera: <u>Siege of Rhodes</u>

1660 Restoration of Charles II

1665–66 Plague and Fire of London

1672 Newton sets out first Law of Gravity

1684 First street lighting in London

1690 Purcell: <u>Dido and Aeneas</u>; <u>Fairy Queen</u>

(top) *George Frideric Handel. Portrait of the composer as a young man by the English painter James Thornhill*

(bottom) *An artist's impression of Bach, surrounded by his family, taking morning prayers*

The age of Bach and Handel (1700–1750)

This period of musical history is dominated by two composers, J. S. Bach and Handel, who were both born in Germany in 1685. Despite their identical year and country of birth, however, they did not both write the same type of music. Handel spent some years early in his life in Italy and his early work was naturally much influenced by what he saw and heard there. After moving to England in 1712, he devoted himself to writing and staging Italian operas in London. Unfortunately, he was not a good business man, and when his opera company failed due to a lack of continuing public support for this style of music, he started writing **oratorios** in

An engraving by the English painter Hogarth of a choir performing Handel's oratorio Judith

English. Although he had further financial problems he was rescued from bankruptcy by his most famous oratorio – *Messiah*. Some of his other oratorios are still performed today – *Israel in Egypt*, *Samson* and *Judas Maccabeus*. He is also remembered for his instrumental music, which includes *Water Music* and *Fireworks Music*.

Bach wrote no operas at all. He did however write much sacred music, some important orchestral music and many keyboard pieces. His work is very **contrapuntal** in style, which means that he tended to write with several melody lines weaving their way in and out of each other. Although Handel's style is often contrapuntal also, he was more inclined to write with a single melody line and an accompaniment. In this way one line of music (the melody) becomes more important than the rest, whereas with **counterpoint** all the lines of music are equally important.

Bach's sacred music includes the *St. Matthew Passion*, the *B Minor Mass* and many **cantatas** (episodes from the Bible set to music for the church). The reason that he wrote so much church music is that he spent much of his life employed in churches as an organist or musical director. After settling in Leipzig in 1723, for example, he was required to write new music for the church services every single

An engraving of the market place, Leipzig, in Bach's time

week. He was a brilliant organist, and wrote many works for the instrument, to be played before and after, and sometimes during, the services. He was also renowned for his improvisation and many of his most famous works including the *Toccata and Fugue in D minor*, were originally improvised.

Bach's instrumental music includes the six *Brandenburg Concertos*. These are known in Italian as 'concerti grossi' (the singular is **concerto grosso**), which are

different in form from the **concertos** of the Classical period and later. In a concerto grosso the orchestra is divided into two sections – a group of soloists and a main body of the orchestra. Handel also composed some concerti grossi and both composers also wrote orchestral and keyboard **suites.** Perhaps Bach's best known keyboard work is the *48 Preludes and Fugues*, in which two **preludes** and two **fugues** are composed in all the major and minor keys.

It should be clear therefore that Bach and Handel were very different both as composers and personalities. Handel travelled around Europe whilst Bach remained in Germany. Bach earned a living by working in churches and for small courts; Handel made his money through the performance of his operas and oratorios.

Finally, two other composers from this period can be mentioned: Alessandro Scarlatti and his son, Domenico. Alessandro wrote over 100 operas in the Italian style, and over 500 chamber **cantatas**, and his development of harmony and form was very important for later composers who built upon his ideas. Domenico was a friend of Handel. In fact, he was born in the same year as Handel and is remembered for over 500 short keyboard sonatas, which did much to develop the technique and style of keyboard composition and performance.

QUESTIONS

1. Three composers were born in 1685. Name them.
2. What type of music did Handel write before turning to the oratorio?
3. What is an oratorio? Name four oratorios by Handel.
4. Although Handel was born in Germany he lived much of his life outside that country. Where did he live?
5. Explain the meaning of **counterpoint**.
6. Name two sacred and two secular works by J. S. Bach.
7. What is a **concerto grosso**?
8. Summarize the main differences between the life and work of Bach and Handel.
9. What sort of music did Alessandro Scarlatti write?
10. Who was Alessandro Scarlatti's son, and what sort of music did he write?

LISTENING

J. S. Bach *Brandenburg Concertos Nos. 1–6* Erato STU 70801/2
   Mass in B minor Vanguard VSD 71190
   St. Matthew Passion RCA LRL 45098
   St. Matthew Passion (excerpts) Decca SXL 322
   World of J. S. Bach (excerpts from various works) Decca SPA 322
   Well Tempered Clavier (48 preludes and fugues) Excerpts DGG 2530 807
   Fantasia and Fugue in G minor, Prelude and Fugue in E minor, Toccata, Adagio and Fugue in C major, Toccata and Fugue in D Minor Philips 6599 368
Handel *Concerti grossi* Op. 3 1–6 Argo ZRG 5400
   Music for the Royal Fireworks/Water Music Philips Universo 6580 147
   Israel in Egypt DGG Archive 2708 020
   Judas Maccabeus Vanguard VCS 10105/7
   Messiah HMV SLS 774
   Messiah (excerpts) Philips 6833 050
   World of Handel (excerpts from various works) Decca SP4 448
D. Scarlatti *Keyboard Sonatas* Erato STU 7200 1

1700

1710
_____
33
C.P.E. Bach 1714-1788

Gluck 1714-1787
34
1720
_____
35
A. Scarlatti 1660- 1725

1730
_____
36
Couperin 1688-1733   Haydn 1732-1809
37

1740
_____
38
Vivaldi 1685-1741

39
1750   J.S.Bach 1685-1750   _____
41
D. Scarlatti 1685-1757   40 47
                              Mozart 1756-1791
Handel 1685-1759 42
1760
_____

1770   43
_____   Beethoven 1770-1827

1780
_____

1790
_____

48
Schubert 1797-1828
1800
_____

1702 First daily English newspaper

1707 Union of England and Scotland

1712 Handel takes up post
     in English court of George I

1715-17 Handel: Water Music

1721 Bach: Brandenburg Concertos

1723 Bach moves to Leipzig

1729 Bach: St Matthew Passion

1738 Bach: B Minor Mass

1739 Handel: Israel in Egypt

1741 Handel: Messiah

1743 Handel: Samson

1746 Handel: Judas Maccabeus

1749 Handel: Fireworks Music

1773 Boston Tea Party

1776 American Declaration of Independence

1786 Mozart: The Marriage of Figaro

1787 Mozart: Don Giovanni

1788 Mozart: G Minor and Jupiter Symphonies

1789 Start of French Revolution
     George Washington first President of USA

1790 Prince Esterházy dies
     leaving Haydn a pension

1791 Haydn completes 12 London Symphonies
     Mozart: The Magic Flute

1799 Haydn: The Creation

1800 Beethoven: 1st Symphony

The Classical period 1750–1800

In recent years the term 'classical' has often been used to mean the opposite to light music or pop music, but in music history it means the musical style which came after the Baroque period and before Romanticism. While the later Romantic ideal was towards individual and personal expression, Classicism here represents music in which form and order were the overriding principles. The aim of the classical composers was for their music to convey a universal feeling of beauty and perfection.

Thus composers of this period became concerned with finding forms of expression best suited to this aim. It was a period of gradual development, not sudden achievement. New forms of music, such as the four-movement **symphony**, did not suddenly appear. They evolved over many years, and were brought to a height by the two great composers of the age – Haydn and Mozart. In their works the classical ideal of beauty of form was developed and perfected.

(left) Franz Joseph Haydn, Austrian composer

(right) Wolfgang Amadeus Mozart, Austrian composer

As with Bach and Handel, the lives of Haydn and Mozart were quite different, but many similarities can be found in their music. Haydn came from a poor background and struggled in early life, but reached old age as an established composer with enough money to secure a comfortable existence. His main job was as a musician to a very wealthy family – the Esterházy family, whose orchestra he directed, and for whom he wrote much of his music. When the head of the family died, Haydn was left a pension which allowed him to travel freely around Europe in his old age, whilst continuing to write music.

Mozart was 24 years younger than Haydn, and although not wealthy, his family was better off. Mozart was recognized as a genius at a very early age. At the age of seven both he and his sister were taken around Europe as child prodigies; that is, children who were able to perform music far better than ordinary children. Mozart thus became very famous for his keyboard performances and compositions early in his life, but as he became older he found it very hard to settle down. Although he later found immediate success with his opera *The Marriage of Figaro*

Title page from a vocal score of Mozart's The Marriage of Figaro. *The picture is a famous scene in the opera where the page, Cherubino, is discovered eaves-dropping on a conversation between the Count, Figaro, and Susanna*

he was quite poor for most of his life. He wrote a great deal of music in his short life (he died at the age of 35), but many of his masterpieces were not fully appreciated by audiences in his lifetime. *Don Giovanni*, the opera he produced immediately after *Figaro*, was too demanding for the audiences of the time. Nevertheless, he was recognized as a genius by Haydn, whose music he admired and with whom he was acquainted.

Haydn was the major force in developing the new classical forms of music, in which Mozart wrote most of his important works. There were four types of instrumental music that both composers were interested in – the **sonata, concerto, string quartet**, and **symphony**. Haydn particularly developed the solo sonata, whilst one of Mozart's main achievements was the development of the classical concerto (not to be confused with the **concerto grosso** of the Baroque period). He wrote concertos for many different solo instruments – among them many for piano and violin.

Both composers wrote many **string quartets** and symphonies, which developed from short pieces of two movements into works of three or four movements written on a much greater scale. Haydn wrote over 100 symphonies, many of the early ones being quite short in comparison with the later, more famous ones. Mozart wrote 41 symphonies, two of the most popular being the *G minor* and the *Jupiter*.

As you might expect, with all this orchestral writing, the orchestra itself changed. By this time it had become the foundation of the orchestra that most Western composers were to use for many years to come. Mozart was the first composer to use the clarinet in the orchestra. In his famous G minor symphony (No. 40) he wrote for the following instruments:

Woodwind Flute, 2 oboes, 2 clarinets, 2 bassoons

Brass 2 horns

Strings 1st violins, 2nd violins, violas, cellos and double basses.

It should be noted that the cello and double bass part were both written on the same line of music. This was because the double bass played the same notes as the cello an octave lower.

Although Haydn wrote many masses his best known choral work was an **oratorio** called *The Creation*. Mozart's best known vocal works are of course his operas, two of which have already been mentioned. He wrote many others including *Così Fan Tutte* and *The Magic Flute*. His best known religious work is the *Requiem*.

A performance of The Creation *in the Grand Hall of the old University of Vienna on 27 March 1808. This was Haydn's last appearance in public before his death the following year. You can see him seated in the centre of the picture*

72

Apart from Haydn and Mozart there are two other composers from this period whose music you may come across – C. P. E. Bach (fifth child of the great J. S. Bach) who wrote much keyboard music, and Gluck, who wrote many operas, the most famous of which is *Orfeo*. He placed a stronger emphasis on the dramatic aspects of opera and this makes his work more realistic than that of other composers of the time.

QUESTIONS

1. Explain the meaning of the word 'classical'.
2. What is a **symphony**?
3. Give the dates and nationalities of the two great composers from this period.
4. What is a child prodigy?
5. What is a **sonata**?
6. What instruments are used to perform a **string quartet**?
7. What woodwind instruments did Mozart use in his Symphony No. 40 in G minor?
8. What is a **clarinet**?
9. Name four operas by Mozart.
10. Name two famous composers, other than Haydn and Mozart, mentioned in this section. What sort of music did they write?

LISTENING

Haydn *Symphonies Nos. 94–104* Decca Ace of Diamonds SDD 503/4/5 (available separately)
   Symphony No. 94 (Surprise), *101* (Clock) Decca SPA 494
   The Creation (in English) HMV SLS 971
   The Creation (highlights) DGG Privilege 2535 146
   String quartet No. 77 DGG SLPM 138886
   Piano sonatas Nos. 6, 10, 18, 20*, 38, 39, 47, 50, 52, 60. Fantasia in C major, Variations in F minor ARGO 1 HDN 100/2
   (NB The numbering of the Haydn sonatas is from the Universal Edition, except that marked * which is from the Haydn Society.)
   Piano sonatas Nos 48, 49, 50, 51. DGG 2530 736
Mozart *Piano Concerto No. 20* (D minor); *23* (A major) Philips 6833 119
   Symphony No. 40 (G minor); *41* (C major, Jupiter) Classics for Pleasure CFP 40253
   Don Giovanni Decca Ace of Diamonds GOS 604–6
   Don Giovanni (highlights) Decca Ace of Diamonds SDD 382
   The Marriage of Figaro Decca Ace of Diamonds GOS 585–7
   The Marriage of Figaro (highlights) Decca Ace of Diamonds SDD 237
   The Magic Flute Decca Ace of Diamonds GOS 501/3
   The Magic Flute (highlights) Decca Ace of Diamonds Decca SPA 251
   The World of Mozart (extracts) Decca SPA 251
   String quartets 14–19 Philips SAL 3632/3/4
   Piano sonatas Nos 8 and 17 Decca SXL 6439
C. P. E. Bach *Sinfonia in F major* and other works Telefunken SAWT 9447
Gluck *Orpheus and Euridice* (highlights) Decca SET 495

MOZART: *Horn Concerto No. 3 in E flat*

1. K447 = a catalogue number. Mozart's works were catalogued by Koechel – hence the abbreviation K.

2. Allegro = fast.

3 and 4. Key signatures. You'll notice that the two key signatures are different. This means that one of the instruments is a transposing instrument. To be quite sure what key the piece is in you can always look at the string section of the orchestra – none of the strings is a transposing instrument.

5. Clarinetti in B = Clarinets in B flat. They sound one tone lower than printed. So the key signature given is one flat – F major, which when transposed down a tone will become E flat major.

6. Fagotti = Bassoons.

7. Corno principale in Es = Solo horn in C. Its notes sound a sixth lower than printed.

8. Violino I = First violins.

9. Violino II = Second violins.

10. Viola = Violas. Notice that the viola part has a viola clef, rather than a treble or bass clef. The middle line is middle C.

11. Violoncello e basso = Cello and double bass. The bass will play one octave lower than the score is printed.

12. C = Common time or $\frac{4}{4}$.

13. ♪ The note should be repeated as if enough semiquavers had been written to last as long as a minim; that is, eight semiquavers.

74

BEETHOVEN: *Symphony No. 7, 2nd movement*

1. Fl. = Flutes.
2. Ob. = Oboes.
3. Cl. = Clarinets.
4. Fag. = Bassoons (from the Italian *fagotto*).
5. Cor = Horns (from the Italian *corno*).
6. Tr. = Trumpets.
7. Timp. = Timpani (or kettle drums).
8. Vl. I = 1st violins.
9. Vl. II = 2nd violins.
10. Vla. = Violas.
11. Vlc. = Cellos (from the full name of the cello – the violoncello).
12. C.B. = Double basses.
13. 90; 100 (at the top and bottom of the score). These are bar numbers.
14. *dimin.* = *diminuendo* (getting softer).
15. *sempre dimin* = softer still.
16. p = soft (from the Italian *piano*).
17. *pizz.* = play these notes with the finger plucking the strings, rather than with the bow. (From the Italian pizzicato.) When the composer wants the cellists and bassists to use the bow again the term *arco* will be written.
18. Three sharps. Beethoven has just modulated to A major and to save writing in the three sharps all the time they now become the new key signature.

75

Beethoven and the early Romantics (1800–1750)

The 19th century is often known as the Romantic period in music. It was a time when composers were concerned with the expression of their own emotions and feelings. They wrote music that appealed to the heart rather than the mind. They also felt that the musical forms that were established in the classical period should be expanded. Many of these concerns reflected the changes that were taking place in art and politics, as the Western world moved away from government by the aristocracy to the early forms of government by the middle classes.

There was, in the 19th century, a belief in freedom and the power of mankind to work things out for itself, and composers were much influenced by this. There was also an interest, by some composers, in literature. This led to the development of a type of music called **programme music**, which was often based on a play, poem or other literary subject. The orchestra grew ever larger. In the 18th century trumpets and horns had been added, and now, at the beginning of the 19th century, trombones as well. Long public concerts were given, with conductors taking over the role of directing the orchestra from the leader of the orchestra, who had previously directed whilst playing.

Beethoven represents the link between the Classical and Romantic periods of music history. He was one of the first composers to be employed neither by the aristocracy nor the church. In his music, he took the classical forms and extended them in many directions. His melodies are perhaps less 'regular' than those of previous composers, and are extended and developed much more fully; his harmonies are more wide-ranging and varied.

Cartoon of Ludwig van Beethoven, German composer

Beethoven met both Mozart and Haydn, and indeed had lessons from Haydn whom he greatly admired. He was a brilliant pianist and during what is generally known as his first period of composition (up to 1802) he wrote a lot of music for the piano. By 1800 the first signs of his deafness had appeared, but he met this tragedy with great courage, and during his middle period (1803–12) wrote the second to eighth symphonies, the fourth and fifth piano concertos and much more. At the end of the middle period, Beethoven was involved in a series of arguments over the custody of his nephew Carl, an affair which worried him very much, and he wrote little at that time. However, by 1820 he was very busy again, and in his last period, during which he was totally deaf, he experimented even further with form, writing his last string quartets, the ninth symphony, and his final piano sonatas. He died in 1827 a very famous composer, recognized as a great genius.

Another composer who bridged the eras of classical and romantic composition was Schubert. His best-known works include his last two symphonies – the *Unfinished* and the *'Great' C major* and many of his songs (he wrote over 500) are famous. Unlike Beethoven he rarely revised his work, and composed without any great struggle. He was the first great German song-writer in a tradition which was continued by Schumann and Brahms.

Franz Liszt; an early photo taken in 1886

During the early Romantic period. the piano became more and more important, with composers like Chopin and Schumann exploring the possibilities of its wide range of expression. The greatest pianist of the period was Liszt, who wrote exciting works which are exceptionally difficult to play. Another composer of the period was Berlioz, who both in life and music represented much that the Romantic movement stood for. In his music, he experimented with the size and composition of the orchestra, often writing for very large ensembles indeed. His most famous work is *Symphonie Fantastique*, a piece of **programme music**, related to a romantic episode from his own life.

Some other composers wrote orchestral works closer to the form of the music of the Classical period – as with Mendelssohn's five symphonies (the most famous being the '*Scotch*' and the '*Italian*') and the four symphonies by Schumann. Mendelssohn also helped develop the **concert overture** – pieces for performance in concerts which were not (as with operatic overtures) introductions to larger musical works. His best known overtures are *Midsummer Night's Dream* and the *Hebrides*.

In the field of opera, one of the most popular composers of the period was Rossini. He wrote *The Barber of Seville* and *William Tell*, which although he lived for a further 39 years after composing it, was his last opera.

Finally, sacred music. This was a period in which there was less interest than previously in religious works. One of the best-known pieces is *Elijah*, an **oratorio** by Mendelssohn.

(left) Manuscript of the Dies Irae *from the* Requiem Mass *by Berlioz. Notice how many instruments the composer uses.*

(right) The Italian composer Gioacchino Rossini set his own name to music

1. What are the main differences between Romantic composers and Classical composers?

2. Which instruments were added to the brass section of the orchestra during this period?

3. How many symphonies did Beethoven write?

4. How did Beethoven represent the link between the Classical and Romantic periods of music history?

5. What tragedy overtook Beethoven at the end of the 18th century?

6. What music is Schubert well remembered for?

7. Name three composers who were interested in developing the possibilities of piano expression.

8. What is **programme music**?

9. Name three pieces of music by Mendelssohn.

10. Who was the most popular operatic composer of the period?

LISTENING   Beethoven *Piano Concerto No. 5*; Egmont Overture Decca Ace of Diamonds SDD 225

Symphonies No. 1 and 2 Philips 6500 113

Symphony No. 3 Decca JB 6

Symphony No. 4; Leonora No. 1 Philips Universo 6580 146

Symphonies Nos. 5 and 8 Classics for Pleasure CFP 40007

Symphony No. 6 Music for Pleasure SIT 60039

Symphony No. 7 Classics for Pleasure CFP 40018

Symphony No. 9 Decca JB1

Piano sonatas ('Pathétique', 'Moonlight', 'Appassionata') HMV HQS 1076

World of Beethoven (extracts) Philips 6833 179

Schubert *Symphony No. 8 ('Unfinished')* Decca SPA 178

Symphony No. 9 Classics for Pleasure CFP 40233

Piano Quintet in A major ('Trout') CBS Classics 61623

Swan Song Decca SXL 6590

World of Schubert (extracts) Decca SPA 426

Berlioz *Symphonie Fantastique* DGG 2530 597

Mendelssohn *Hebrides; Midsummer Night's Dream* Decca SPA 92

Symphonies 3 and 4 ('Scotch' and 'Italian') Decca SXL 6363

Rossini *Barber of Seville* (highlights) Decca SXL 6271

William Tell HMV SLS 6271

World of Rossini (extracts) Decca SPA 445

1800

Berlioz 1803-1869

Mendelssohn 1809-1847

Chopin 1810-1849

Schumann 1810-1856

Haydn 1732-1809

1810

Liszt 1811-1886

Wagner 1813-1883

Verdi 1813-1901

1820

Smetana 1824-1884

Beethoven 1770-1827

Schubert 1797-1828

1830

Brahms 1833-1897

1840

Tchaikovsky 1840-1893

Dvořák 1841-1904

Grieg 1843-1907

Rimsky-Korsakov 1844-1908

1850

Elgar 1857-1934

1860

Debussy 1862-1918

Sibelius 1865-1957

Rossini 1792-1868

1870

Vaughan Williams 1872-1958

Holst 1874-1934

1880

Stravinsky 1882-1971

1890

1900

1800 Beethoven: <u>1st Symphony</u>

1804 Beethoven: <u>Eroica Symphony</u>

1809 Beethoven: <u>Emperor Concerto</u>

1816 Schubert: <u>The Erl King</u>

1816 Rossini: <u>The Barber of Seville</u>

1822 Schubert: <u>Unfinished Symphony</u>

1824 Beethoven: <u>9th Symphony</u>

1826 Mendelssohn: <u>A Midsummer Night's Dream</u>

1828 Schubert: <u>C Major Symphony</u>

1829 Mendelssohn: <u>'Scotch' Symphony;</u>

  <u>The Hebrides</u>

1829 Rossini: <u>William Tell</u>

1832 Berlioz: <u>Fantastic Symphony</u>

1833 Mendelssohn: <u>Italian Symphony</u>

1843 Wagner: <u>Flying Dutchman</u>

1846 Mendelssohn: <u>Elijah</u>

1851-53 Verdi: <u>Rigoletto;</u>

  <u>Il Trovatore; La Traviata</u>

1865 Brahms: <u>A German Requiem</u>

1866 Smetana: <u>Bartered Bride</u>

1868 Grieg: <u>A Minor Piano Concerto</u>

1876 Wagner: First Festival at Bayreuth.

  <u>The Ring</u> performed

1877 Brahms: <u>2nd Symphony</u>

1877 Tchaikovsky: <u>4th Symphony</u>

1879 Brahms: <u>Academic Festival Overture</u>

1882 Tchaikovsky: <u>1812 Overture</u>

1883 Brahms: <u>3rd Symphony</u>

1885 Brahms: <u>4th Symphony</u>

1888 Rimsky- Korsakov: <u>Scheherazade</u>

1892 Dvořák: Symphony <u>'From the New World'</u>

1892 Debussy: <u>A L'Après-midi d'un Faune</u>

1899 Sibelius: <u>Finlandia</u>

1899 Elgar: <u>Enigma Variations</u>

1900 Elgar: <u>The Dream of Gerontius</u>

1804 Napoleon becomes Emperor of France

1805 Battle of Trafalgar

1815 Battle of Waterloo

1820-1910 Florence Nightingale

1821-25 Stockton-Darlington Railway built

1837 Dickens: <u>Oliver Twist</u>

1837 Victoria becomes Queen

1840 Penny Post introduced

1841 Saxophone invented

1848 Marx and Engels: Communist Manifesto

1859 Darwin: <u>Origin of the Species</u>

1860 Abraham Lincoln becomes President of USA

1864 First London Underground Line opened

1865 Lewis Carroll: <u>Alice in Wonderland</u>

1875 Mark Twain: <u>Tom Sawyer</u>

1876 Telephone invented

1880 First practical electric light developed

1889 Eiffel Tower opened

1889-1945 Adolf Hitler

1890 Free elementary education in England

1891 Conan Doyle: <u>Adventures of Sherlock Holmes</u>

1893 First car developed

1897 H.G.Wells: <u>The Invisible Man</u>

The later Romantics 1850–1900

The second half of the 19th century saw the Romantic movement split into two parts. There were composers who wrote in the tradition of the Classical period (although their music still reflects some of the new ideas of the century). There were also those who followed the new directions offered by Liszt and Berlioz. Brahms is the best known composer in the first category, and Wagner the best known in the second.

At the same time there was a trend towards nationalism in music, following the influence of Napoleon and the awakening of people's political awareness. Strong nationalist schools arose in several countries. Liszt, for example, wrote a number of Hungarian dances, and Chopin wrote Polish dances. In Russia, a group of five composers met together in order to establish an easily identifiable Russian style of music. Best known of these five was Rimsky-Korsakov, who wrote the orchestral **tone-poem** *Scheherazade*. Tchaikovsky, the best known of all the composers from Russia at this time, was not a member of this group. He did not seek deliberately to put Russian influences such as folk-song themes into his music, but he did develop a style which is distinctly Russian.

Two other nationalist composers may be mentioned here – Smetana from Bohemia (now Czechoslovakia), who wrote operas in his native language (including *The Bartered Bride*), and Grieg from Norway who made great use of his country's folk music and folk stories.

Scene from Smetana's opera The Bartered Bride

Wagner, the most important German opera composer of the period, was also a nationalist in some senses, as he used subjects from German myths and legends as the basis for his operas, or **music dramas** as he called them. Wagner believed deeply in the unity of the arts through music drama, in which acting, dancing, music, poetry, singing and stage craft could all be equally combined. He wrote both music and words for his music dramas and directed performances himself in a theatre that he designed specifically for his works at Bayreuth. In his works, Wagner added to and extended the use of the orchestra. He also introduced the 'leitmotive' – a theme which recurs throughout an opera (in the voice parts, or, more commonly, in the orchestra), and which is always associated with one particular event, action or character. This technique was used most extensively in *The Ring of the Nibelung*, a cycle of four music dramas – *The Rhinegold, The Valkyrie, Siegfried*, and *Twilight of the Gods*. Also important are the large-scale works *The Mastersingers* and *Tristan and Isolde*, and the popular opera *The Flying Dutchman*, which, earlier in his life, had set him on the road to success.

Of course, Wagner was not the only operatic composer during this period. The Italian opera tradition continued and was further developed by Giuseppe Verdi. He combined the traditional Italian gift for flowing and tuneful melodies with a deeper feeling for the dramatic aspects of opera. Three of his most popular works were written between 1851 and 1853 – *Rigoletto, Il Trovatore*, and *La Traviata* – but quite as important were *Aida, Otello*, and *Falstaff*. These last two mentioned operas were written late in his life, and were both based on plays by Shakespeare. At a time when everyone was talking about Wagner and his music dramas, these works showed the Italian public how opera could develop on alternative lines, still according to Italian traditions.

Brahms was also seen by many people as continuing a tradition – that of the orchestral music of Beethoven. Wagner also claimed to be writing in this tradition, arguing that in his ninth symphony Beethoven had been reaching towards a unity of music and words – a unity which he, Wagner, then achieved. Brahms wrote four symphonies, as well as other orchestral works such as the *Academic Festival Overture*, plus chamber music, songs, piano music and one of the major sacred works of this period – *A German Requiem*. This work, as the name suggests, is very much in the Germanic tradition, and is thus in complete contrast to the best-known sacred work of the period, the *Requiem* by Verdi, which reflects the tragic and dramatic power of his operas.

Tchaikovsky wrote six symphonies, of which the last three are best known. He also wrote some programme music, including the famous *1812* overture and the Fantasy-overture *Romeo and Juliet*. Some of his most popular music was written for ballet, such as *Swan Lake*, the *Nutcracker* suite, and *Sleeping Beauty*.

Lastly, mention must be made of Dvořák, whose most often played work today is his *New World Symphony*. He followed the tradition of Brahms in his composition and added to it his own awareness of his Czechoslovakian roots. Apart from his symphonies, his chamber music is also much appreciated today.

QUESTIONS

1. Name one composer who developed the tradition of the Classical period between 1850 and 1900.

2. Name one composer who followed the direction of composition of Liszt and Berlioz during this period.

3. Who was the most famous Russian composer of this period? Name one piece of ballet music and one piece of programme music by him.

4. Name four nationalist composers and state the nationality of each.

5. What is a **tone poem**?

6. What subjects did Wagner use as the basis for his compositions?

7. What is a **leitmotive** and who introduced the idea?

8. What is a music drama? Why do you think this title is particularly appropriate to the operas of Wagner?

9. Where is the theatre that was built to stage the works of Wagner?

10. Name two orchestral works by Brahms, other than his symphonies.

LISTENING

Liszt *Hungarian Rhapsodies (G244)* DGG 2530 441

Rimsky-Korsakov *Scheherazade* HMV SXLP 20026

Tchaikovsky *1812 Overture; Marche Slave; Romeo and Juliet* HMV ASD 2894

  Symphony No. 4 DGG 2530 651

  Symphony No. 5 CBS Classics 61289

  Symphony No. 6 Philips 6500 081

  Swan lake (highlights) Decca SXL 2285

  Swan Lake (complete) Decca 10BB 168/70

  Sleeping Beauty (highlights) HMV ASD3370

Smetana *Ma Vlast; Overture to The Bartered Bride* etc. HMV SXLP 30199

Wagner *Overtures* CBS Classics 61263

The Flying Dutchman (highlights) Decca Ace of Diamonds SDD 439

Greatest Hits CBS Harmony 30008

Brahms *Academic Festival Overture; Tragic Overture; Var. on Theme by Haydn* CBS Classics 61784

Symphony No. 1 HMV SXLP 30217

World of Brahms Decca SPA 315

Verdi *World of Verdi* Decca SPA 447

Requiem Mass HMV SLS909

Dvořák *Symphony No. 9 in E minor ('From the New World')* DGG SLPM 138922

Favourite Composer (collection) Decca DPA 539/40

Grieg *Piano Concerto in A minor* Philips 6500 166

The 20th century (1900–1945)

In the 20th century, up to the end of the Second World War, four different styles of composition may be distinguished: nationalist, impressionist, neo-romantic and anti-romantic. At the same time the rise of new technology led to such inventions as the gramophone and, much later, the tape recorder, although it was not until after the Second World War that composers were really influenced by these developments.

Nevertheless, pre-war compositions do reflect a world which was changing faster than ever before, as composers developed many new techniques of composition. This has meant that, although some works from the 20th century are very popular in the concert hall today, a lot of the more experimental pieces have not found the same popularity, largely because they are so different from what most people regard as 'normal'.

In the 20th century English music achieved world importance again, after many years of relative obscurity. After the death of Purcell in 1695 there were no English composers comparable to Haydn, Mozart and Beethoven. But after the end of the 19th century a number of English composers emerged – Elgar, Vaughan Williams, Holst, (and later, Walton and Britten) – whose work reflected the nationalist movements of the previous century, and who established a truly British character

LUDGATE HILL & CIRCUS FROM FLEET STREET. 4523.

(opposite) *Fleet Street, London, at the end of the 19th century. A scene like this could have inspired Vaughan Williams's* London Symphony

(left) *Ralph Vaughan Williams, English composer, in his study*

(right) *Claude Debussy; French composer much influenced by the Impressionist movement*

in their music. It was Vaughan Williams who led the way, by collecting and using a large number of English folk songs from various parts of the country, which until then had been largely neglected.

In France a school of painting had grown up towards the end of the 19th century called Impressionism, where the immediate impression of a scene was more important than the details. The resulting 'dreaminess', pictures with subtle touches of colour and light, is typical of such painters as Renoir, Monet, and Cézanne. Debussy was much influenced by this development. In his impressionist compositions, he tried to represent an overall effect, full of orchestral colour and light, rather than depicting any particular detail. This can be seen in such works as *La Mer*, in which the subject is the sea, in various aspects, and the *Prélude à l'après-midi d'un faune*.

The neo- (or new) romantics, on the other hand, carried further the traditions of the romantic period. The composers in this group included Sibelius who combined neo-romanticism with a nationalism reflecting his feelings about his country, Finland, and its domination by Russia. His **tone-poem** *Finlandia* was, in fact, banned by the Russian government, which then ruled Finland. Much of his best work is, however, contained in his seven symphonies.

Vaughan Williams also coupled romanticism and nationalism, as well as taking an interest in music from the 16th century and earlier, as in his *G minor Mass*, and the famous *Tallis Fantasia*. He wrote nine symphonies, all of which are performed regularly today. The seventh, the *Sinfonia Antartica*, was used as music for the film *Scott of the Antarctic*, though perhaps his best-known symphony is the *London Symphony*. The influence of folk song can be seen in such a work as the *Fantasia on Greensleeves*.

89

Elgar also wrote in a neo-romantic style. One of his most popular works is the *Enigma Variations* for orchestra (musical 'portraits' of his friends). He also wrote two symphonies and several important choral works, such as *The Dream of Gerontius*. Although he was not particularly interested in English folk music he did write some very 'English' music, such as the *Pomp and Circumstance* marches, some of which were written for Royal occasions and which convey aptly the mood of Edwardian England.

The anti-romantic composers branched out in different directions. They wanted to move beyond the simple, regular meters of the classical and romantic tradition, and sought to develop new ideas of melody, rhythm, and harmony. The folk music of Eastern Europe had always made use of unusual rhythm and harmonies (for example, the use of modes, five beats to a bar etc). In this period such devices became used more often in larger-scale works, as a reaction against romantic music. The leading anti-romantic composer was a Russian: Stravinsky.

Stravinsky at work in his study in Los Angeles in 1961

Stravinsky experimented with such ideas as combining two unrelated keys (polytonality) or two or more different rhythms (polyrhythm) at the same time. At first audiences found this hard to listen to, and some of his early works were very badly received. *The Rite of Spring* actually caused a riot at its first performance. But besides looking forward with radical developments such as these, he also used musical forms from the 18th century and combined them with 20th-century musical ideas, as in his *Symphony of Psalms*. This treatment of classical forms with 20th-century ideas is the basis of neo-classicism.

The Austrian composer Schoenberg started writing as a neo-romantic. He developed even further the extreme chromatic harmonies that Wagner had used, in such works as *Verklärte Nacht* or the **song-cycle** *Pierrot Lunaire*. He realized, however, that there was a limit to the possibilities of this type of romantic expression, and that this limit had been reached. Other composers had also realized this, and reacted in various ways. Stravinsky, as we have seen, turned either to polytonality and polyrhythm or back to the 18th century for inspiration. And Debussy developed a technique based on the **whole-tone scale** (i.e., A, B, C sharp, D sharp, F, G). Schoenberg, however, developed a radically new idea – that of **serial composition**, where a piece is based on a 12-note theme in which no note is repeated. The resulting piece has no key or scale and is still very difficult to understand today.

In America, a school of composers became established that incorporated many of the different styles that had developed in Europe. The best known composers of this school were Charles Ives, Aaron Copland and George Gershwin. It was Gershwin who added elements of jazz and blues to his music, most notably in *Rhapsody in Blue* and the folk-opera *Porgy and Bess*.

Thus, in the years up to 1945, many new and different approaches to musical composition emerged. However, all these developments had a common cause. They all represented a search for new modes of musical expression. After 1945 this search was taken up by a new group of composers.

QUESTIONS
1. Name five English composers from this period.
2. What was Vaughan Williams's connection with folk music?
3. Name a leading impressionist composer.
4. What tradition does neo-romanticism seek to continue?
5. What nationality was Sibelius, and name two works by him.
6. Name one work by Vaughan Williams.
7. What nationality was Elgar? Name three of his compositions.
8. Explain the difference between the neo-romantics and the anti-romantics.
9. What is **serial composition** and who helped develop it?
10. What is the **whole tone scale**? Name one composer who used it in his compositions.

LISTENING
Elgar *Favourite Composer* Decca DPA 527/8
   Greatest Hits CBS Harmony 30055
   Pomp and Circumstance Marches DGG Privilege 2535 217
   Enigma Variations HMV ASD 2750
Vaughan Williams *Sinfonia Antartica* HMV ASD 2631
Holst *The Planets* Decca Ace of Diamonds SDD 400
Walton *Façade* Decca Eclipse ECS 586
Britten *The World of Britten* (excerpts) Decca SPA 74
   Peter Grimes (highlights) Decca SXL 2309
Debussy *Prélude à l'après-midi d'un faune; La Mer* CBS 73533
Sibelius *Finlandia; Karelia suite* HMV ASD 2272
Stravinsky *The Rite of Spring* CBS 72807
   Symphony of Psalms CBS 72181
Schoenberg *Serenade* Oiseau Lyre SOL 250

all one back,

1900	Verdi 1813–1901 99	100
	Dvořák 1841–1904 102	Walton 1902–
	Grieg 1843–1907 103	
1910	Rimsky-Korsakov 1844–1908 104	Messiaen 1908– 125
		Cage 1912– 106
		Britten 1913–1976 130
	Debussy 1862–1918 110	108
1920		
		Boulez 1925– 113
		Berio 1925– 114
1930		Stockhausen 1928– 116
	Holst 1874–1934 118	Penderecki 1933– 117
	Elgar 1857–1934 119	Cardew 1936–
1940		
1950		
	Schoenberg 1871–1951 123	
	Vaughan Williams 1872–1958 125	
1960		
1970		
	Stravinsky 1882–1971 128	
1980		

1900 Elgar: The Dream of Gerontius

1903 First flight by Wright Brothers

1913 First symphony recorded

1913 Stravinsky: The Rite of Spring   1914-18 First World War

1920 Holst: The Planets

1922 Vaughan Williams: Pastoral Symphony   1922 BBC formed

1924 Lenin dies, Stalin takes control in USSR

1926 First sound movie. General strike in UK

1930 Stravinsky: Symphony of Psalms

1932 Very high unemployment

1935-77 Elvis Presley

1939-45 Second World War

1948 First LP produced

1951 Britten: Billy Budd   1952 First hydrogen bomb exploded

1953 Vaughan Williams:

     Sinfonia Antartica (no.7)   1958 Stereo records become available

1954 Bill Haley: Rock around the Clock   1961 First man in space: Yuri Gargarin

1961 Britten: War Requiem

1971 Stockhausen: Hymnen   1971 First man lands on the moon

1945 to the present day

In this book you have read about some of the many changes in musical composition since 1550. Each period of music has had its own particular type of composition. However, in the 20th century, the speed of change has become much faster than ever before. As a result, many composers have often found that at first people did not like their music or understand it, although they sometimes have come to be recognized as great musicians later on. Music written since the end of the Second World War (1945) is even harder to understand. Some of this music, in fact, appears to be totally different from everything that has gone before.

Why has modern music developed in this way? There are two possible answers. First, modern music may only sound unusual because we don't hear very much of it. If we listened to it a lot more it would not seem so strange.

The second possible answer is that much of the music written since 1945 has changed so much in style from the classical and romantic tradition that it is no longer related to it at all. Since the avant-garde, as some of this post-war music is called, is something completely new, it should not be compared with the music of, for example, Beethoven. Some writers have thus argued that the musical styles you have read about in this book have now come to an end, i.e. the tradition of music that developed after 1600 ended with the many new developments described in the section *1900–1945*. But why has this change happened now, and why so rapidly? It is often argued that music is changing so rapidly because life itself is changing so much. In 1600 life for most people was not very different from the lives of people who had lived a hundred years earlier. But life in the 1980s is very different from life only 30 years ago. Things are changing faster than ever before, and so it is not surprising that music is also changing very quickly.

No one knows for certain what is happening to 'serious' music at the moment. It is not even certain that it will continue to change so fast. Not all music written since 1945 has been in the experimental style of avant-garde composers. Britten, Tippett, Stravinsky, Shostakovich, Vaughan Williams and many other composers continued to develop the forms and styles described in previous sections of this book. It is impossible to know at the moment if the most important developments in music will result from the avant-garde, the neo-romantics, the anti-romantics or even pop music.

Below are a few notes about eight leading avant-garde composers. You can read about developments in pop music in the next section.

Luciano Berio An Italian who has written electronic and orchestral music. Some of his pieces leave the performers to choose which order to play the notes in.
Pierre Boulez A French composer who is also famous as a conductor. He is interested in the mathematical relationships between sounds, and has written complicated pieces for piano, again with some decisions left to the performer.

John Cage An American well known for his works for the **prepared piano** in which objects are placed inside the piano in order to change the sounds made, and for **aleatory** pieces in which the sounds are completely random. He has also written music in which what he writes is determined by the slight marks already existing on the manuscript paper.

Cornelius Cardew English composer at one time associated with Stockhausen, but now developing a musical language which he sees as a suitable way of expressing what he considers to be the workers' struggle against oppression. He developed the Scratch Orchestra for musicians and non-musicians to perform and compose together.

Peter Maxwell Davies An English composer whose early works showed the influence of **Serialism** and the rhythmic experiments of Messiaen (see below). Since the early 1970s he has lived in Orkney and his music reflects life there. He has also written music for films by Ken Russell, (for example *The Devils*).

Olivier Messiaen A Frenchman influenced by the music of India, and as a result much of his work is very complicated rhythmically. He also uses birdsong extensively in his music, much of which is religious in spirit.

Olivier Messiaen, French composer

Krzystof Penderecki A Polish composer who has written religious and operatic music, who is noted for his use of 'sound blocks', in which the performers are instructed to play in a certain way within a period of time, but not necessarily all together.

Karlheinz Stockhausen A German composer who has been one of the main developers of **electronic music**. He has been particularly noted for the use of **indeterminacy** in his music, although many of his works are based on very precise mathematical relationships, reflecting his fascination with numbers. He has also experimented with **spatial effects**.

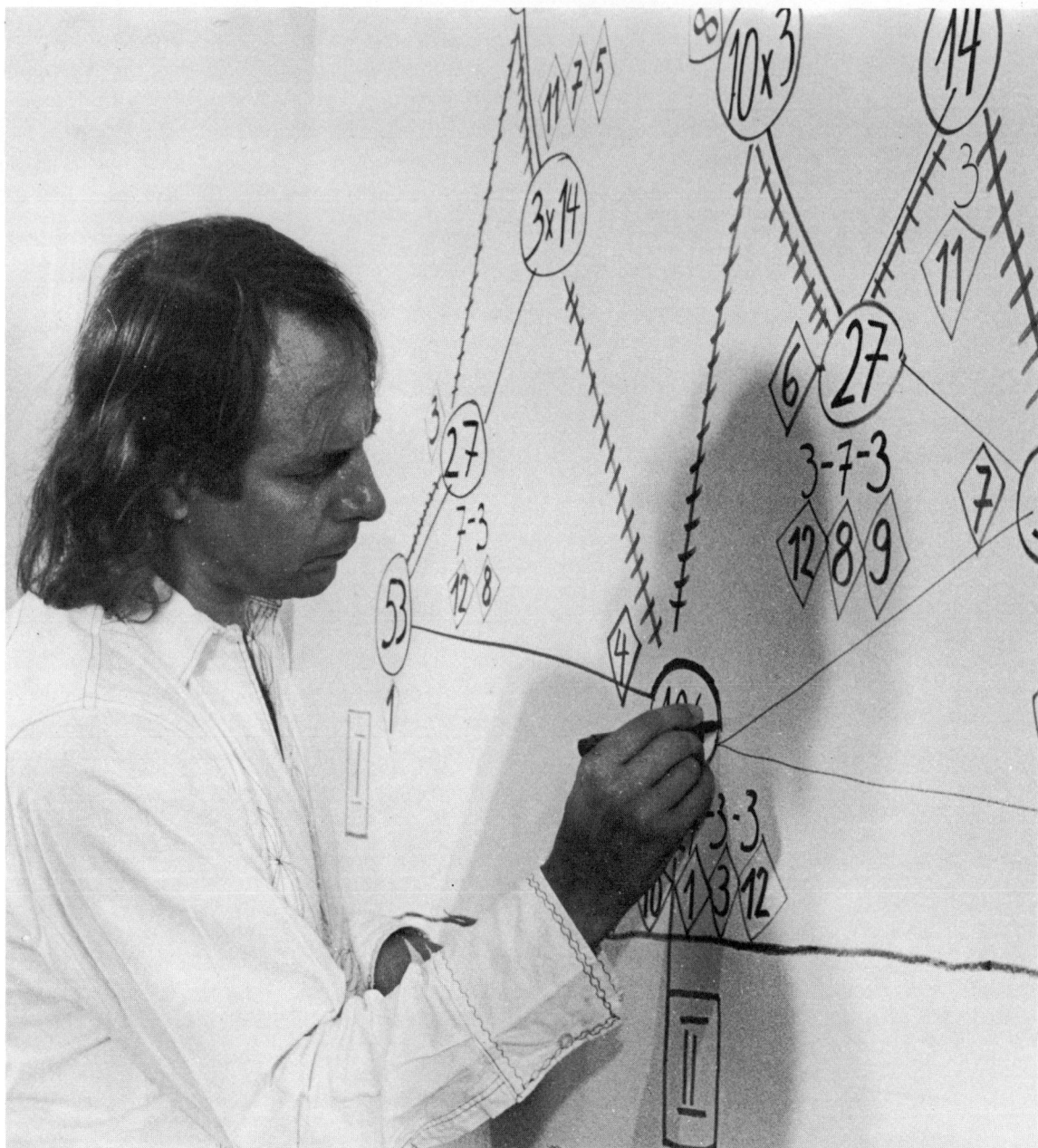

Stockhausen preparing a graph of his composition Mantra *before a lecture*

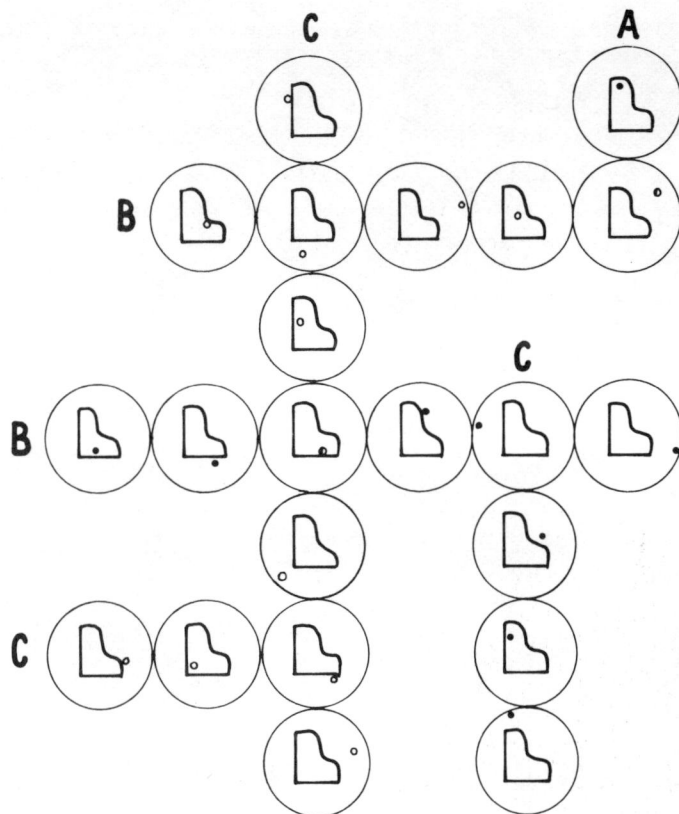

CORNELIUS CARDEW:

Memories of You (Piano Solo)

Each circle gives the location of a sound relative to a grand piano. The sound should begin and/or end at the point indicated.

Durations and dynamics are free, and so are total time and points of entry of all sounds within that time.

All sounds are to be played once only. Circles forming horizontal chains are to occur in the order given (reading from left to right); those forming vertical chains may be read in any order.

Every chain has a letter affixed to it. These letters (A, B, C) refer to any three objects for making sounds. Thus, all sounds in a chain headed B are to be made with the object B. (Suggested objects: side drum or bass drum stick, matchbox, comb, hand, glass ashtray, plastic lid, etc.)

Where a sound occurs at the intersection of two chains by different letters, both objects are to be used in making the sound.

The pedal may be engaged throughout the piece.

Sounds made at floor level are indicated by ●.

Sounds made above floor level are indicated by ○.

Sounds made both on the floor and above the floor are indicated by ◐.

97

Music and the listener today

(top) Benjamin Britten (centre) rehearsing at The Maltings, Snape, where the Aldeburgh music festival takes place. Left to right: the singer Peter Pears, Britten, the conductor and composer André Previn, and the singer Elisabeth Söderström

(bottom) The conductor Colin Davis facing an enthusiastic audience at the last night of the Proms, Royal Albert Hall, London

Music currently plays a larger part in the lives of people in this country than at any time in the past. So far we have only considered the music *written* since 1945. It is also important to consider what is being *listened* to today.

Although the work of the avant-garde composers mentioned in the previous section is sometimes performed, most of the concerts given, and most of the recordings made, are of pieces written before 1945, or of newly-composed pop music.

There are three main ways in which people can hear music – on the radio, on records, and at concerts. The radio station which broadcasts all kinds of 'serious' music, from the classical-romantic tradition to the avant-garde, as well as early music, is B.B.C. Radio 3. You will find full details of all its broadcasts in the *Radio Times*. If you want to know about records you can either buy a record catalogue from a large record store, or else visit a record library – most large towns have one attached to the main public library.

Apart from the concert halls in most large towns and cities, which provide an opportunity for people to hear 'serious' music, there are also a number of festivals organized each year. These festivals may last for anything from a few days to a month. They give local people a chance to hear some of the finest music played by the best musicians, and also attract tourists to the town. This means that the local traders and hoteliers do extra business, which they obviously welcome. Listed below are some of the festivals held annually in Britain.

Aldeburgh: specializes in music by Britten and new music by other British composers, although rarely avant-garde music. Also includes some early music.

Bath: usually includes music by Sir Michael Tippett.

Cardiff: emphasis on 20th-century music – especially that of Welsh composers.

Cheltenham: concentrates on contemporary British music, but includes much other work.

Edinburgh: an international festival covering all the arts. The music ranges from opera to symphonies.

Glyndebourne: an operatic 'season', usually including works by most major opera composers, particularly Mozart.

The Proms: the most famous English festival, held in the Royal Albert Hall in London and founded by Sir Henry Wood. It covers a wide range of music including contemporary works, and sometimes some avant-garde pieces. Much of the music is broadcast live by the BBC on radio and television.

Three Choirs: alternates between Gloucester, Worcester and Hereford – the music being performed in the cathedrals of each city. Includes new works by English composers.

In addition there are also many competition festivals held – such as the Welsh Eisteddfod, and the Leeds International Piano Competition.

Many festivals are held in Europe – two of the most famous being at Salzburg (Austria) where the festival always includes works by Mozart (who was born in Salzburg) and Bayreuth (Germany) whose performances of Wagner's operas are given in a theatre designed by Wagner especially for this purpose.

QUESTIONS
1. Give two reasons why modern music sometimes sounds very unusual to many people today.

2. What reason could be given for the rapid changes taking place in music at the moment?

3. Name three composers who have written music since the Second World War that is not in the avant-garde tradition.

4. Name two French avant-garde composers.

5. What is a **prepared piano**?

6. What is the meaning of **aleatory** when used to describe pieces of music?

7. Which composer developed an orchestra for musicians and non-musicians to work together?

8. What is **indeterminacy**?

9. Name three important ways of hearing music today.

10. Name three festivals that always include some contemporary British music.

LISTENING
Berio *Recital 1* RCA SER 5665
Boulez *Le Marteau sans Maître* CBS 73213
Cage *Concerto for prepared piano* Nonesuch H71201
Messiaen *L'Ascension* Argo ZRG 5339
Penderecki *Magnificat* EMI EMD 5524
Stockhausen *Stimmung* DGG 2543 003
Hymnen Kontakte Vox STGBY 638

Pop music since 1950

There has always been popular music: it didn't suddenly start in 1950. However, just as 1550 is a convenient date to start a history of music, so 1950 is a convenient date to begin talking about 'pop' music, for it is only since then that most of the pop records that you can hear on the radio have been made.

Pop music comes from a completely different tradition from that of the music written by, say Bach, Mozart and Beethoven. There has always been music for the ordinary people. It often took the form of love songs, or dance music. Pop music is the modern version of this long tradition. From time to time a work by a pop composer has certain similarities to a piece written by a 'serious' composer and occasionally a work from the classical-romantic repertoire becomes a piece of pop music, usually rearranged. But generally the two traditions are quite separate.

However, in recent years some pop composers have been developing a style of music which seems to be taking them nearer to modern developments in the classical tradition. Indeed, a future edition of this book might include them in the chapter on music from 1945 to the present day, rather than in a separate chapter on pop music.

SKIFFLE AND ROCK 'N' ROLL

These were the names given to two forms of music that were popular in the late 1950s. The main skiffle artist in Britain was Lonnie Donegan who had a lot of success with very simple records on which he played the guitar and sang, accompanied by a second guitar, drums, and double bass. It was Donegan who helped to make the guitar a popular instrument in this country.

Rock 'n' roll was a much bigger craze than skiffle and included such names as Bill Haley (who made *Rock around the Clock* in 1954) and Elvis Presley, the most

Bill Haley and his Comets rehearsing for their first London show in 1957

Elvis Presley shooting his film Loving You *in 1957*

famous of all the pop stars of the age. Both artists took a type of music common to black musicians in America called **rhythm and blues**, and combined it with styles that were already popular, such as **country and western**, to produce rock 'n' roll. However, Presley quickly moved away from this style and produced many ballads, love songs and even religious songs.

THE BEATLES

Most of the Beatles' music was written by John Lennon and Paul McCartney, and their songs have become very famous and highly regarded. It has even been suggested that they continued the song tradition started by Schubert. Lennon and

102

*The Beatles'
first film,* A
Hard Day's
Night, *at the
London Pavilion*

McCartney took the simple pop song and developed it using far more subtle chord sequences, melodies and harmonies than ever before. Many of their lyrics are totally unrelated to previous topics for pop songs, often being about characters and situations, sometimes real, sometimes invented. Between 1964 and 1970 their style of music was very varied and every album produced was different in style from the one before – something that most pop stars are unable to risk doing for fear of losing popularity.

BOB DYLAN

Bob Dylan has had perhaps more influence on the history of pop music than any other single person. He first came to fame through records of his own compositions on which he accompanied himself with a guitar and harmonica. Such songs as *Don't think twice, it's all right* and *Blowing in the Wind* quickly became known world wide – particularly because of their lyrics. Indeed, many people saw Dylan as a poet rather than as a musician.

Virtually every pop musician whose music has remained popular for more than two or three years will admit to having been influenced in some way by Dylan. His style of singing (totally different from anyone else's) has often been criticized, as have his continual changes of musical style, but, generally speaking, each record that he has produced has, sooner or later, made its mark on the development of pop music.

PAUL SIMON

Paul Simon comes from the same tradition as Bob Dylan – he started out as a folk singer accompanying himself on an acoustic guitar. He rose to fame in 1965 when Bob Dylan suddenly changed from appearing on stage alone to working with a

103

Bob Dylan with electric guitar – 1970s' style

rock group and singing what is now known as folk-rock. By that time Paul Simon had made a number of unsuccessful records, but a producer took one of them – *Sound of Silence* – added a folk-rock backing and the record became a big hit.

Since then Simon has written a large number of very successful songs, including *Bridge over Troubled Water*, (one of a number of records he made with Art Garfunkel), and he remains popular.

ROCK

The Rolling Stones, like the Beatles, were influenced in the early 60s by rhythm and blues music, but they developed their own style, much harsher than that of the Beatles, and wrote a number of very famous songs – such as *Satisfaction*. Their music has often reflected the side of life that most pop songs ignore – failure, drug addiction, depression, and so on. Although they have continued to make records during recent years, these have not been as successful as their earlier hits.

The work of groups like The Rolling Stones was even further developed by Jimi Hendrix, whose music seemed to take pop closer and closer to the work of the avant-garde composers dealing in **electronic music**. His new developments in guitar technique caught the attention of many well known pop stars who went to watch his concert performances. He appeared to reach his peak in 1968 and after that his music started to lose some of its originality. He died in 1970, aged 28.

The Who originated at the same time as the Rolling Stones, but took rock music in a different direction. Although at first developing the idea that destruction could be artistic (they often demolished their guitars and drums on stage) they are now best known for the double LP and film *Tommy*, sometimes called a pop opera, but better described as a type of **song cycle**. This was followed by another 'song cycle' *Quadrophenia*, which although musically one of the most advanced pieces of pop of the time, has received less wide recognition by music critics.

BLACK MUSIC IN THE 60S AND 70S

Three types of black music have become popular in recent years: soul, reggae and Tamla Motown. Soul music comes from gospel music – black religious songs. The word 'soul' now means music that has a certain honesty about it: it is music about real feelings, sung by people who believe what they are singing about. The most important soul singers have been Otis Redding, James Brown, Curtis Mayfield and Wilson Pickett. Their work influenced the Beatles and Rolling Stones in their early days.

Reggae is pop music from Jamaica which became popular in England with the growth of black communities in English cities. The songs are always about important aspects of Jamaican life, and are easily recognizable by the heavy emphasis of the second and fourth beat in every bar of four beats. The emphasis is so heavy that sometimes the first and third notes are left out altogether.

Tamla Motown is the name of the world's biggest black-owned record company. Among the people who have recorded for Motown are The Miracles, The Temptations, Diana Ross The Jacksons, and Stevie Wonder. The aim of the company has been to develop the music of black singers so that they appeal to white audiences as well, and in this they have been very successful indeed.

PROGRESSIVE ROCK

Many people who like top 20 pop find progressive rock very hard to understand or listen to. This is music that is to be found on LPs by such groups as Pink Floyd, Frank Zappa and the Mothers of Invention, and Yes. The term is also used to describe the work of such individual performers as Mike Oldfield.

Pink Floyd produced a number of interesting LPs between 1967 and 1971 relating to various fantasy themes – such as the idea of escape on flying saucers. In 1973 they produced *The Dark Side of the Moon*, an LP which has now sold over four million copies and which differs from all their previous work. It is concerned with the fears of growing old, of being poor and lonely, and above all, the fear of going mad. This record completely rejects all the hopes of making a better world that many young pop musicians of the 60s expressed in their music.

In the same year another important record was made: *Tubular Bells* by Mike Oldfield. Oldfield played all the instruments on the record himself, and recorded them, one track on top of the next. This record was immediately very popular. Many artists followed up this idea of an album consisting of one long piece of music, all of it recorded by just one person.

Frank Zappa is an American regarded by many as the most brilliant composer of pop music today. He has been deeply influenced by many 20th-century composers of orchestral music (most notably Stravinsky), and has adapted their ideas to fit pop music. His music is often far too difficult for most pop musicians to play, and many have criticized him for this. All of Zappa's work is related, so that ideas and themes from one LP often turn up on another record, released at another time. It can in fact be argued that Zappa is simply writing one long piece of music which is developed further with each new album.

Yes, a British progressive rock group, perform what is called 'symphonic rock'. Although they play pop instruments they have tried to organize some of their pieces as in the classical way, which makes them very different from the conventional two and a half minute pop song.

FUTURE DEVELOPMENTS

The world of pop music moves very quickly, and it is quite possible for a new fashion to become popular within a matter of a few weeks. However, it is difficult to know if that fashion will lead anywhere, or if the music will be forgotten as soon as the records in that style leave the top 50 charts. Writing this in 1980 it is possible to make predictions – but of course these could be completely wrong.

A recent craze is punk rock – which in itself seems to be going nowhere. But even punk has led to a new style of music, 'New Wave', which seems to be a combination of music about everyday things (as in punk) and the musical styles of progressive rock of the late 1960s. This could lead to other equally interesting developments – although probably under a different name. Only time will tell.

QUESTIONS
1. Explain some of the differences between pop music and the music of the classical-romantic tradition.

2. How did Lennon and McCartney develop the pop song?

3. Which pop composer and performer has been thought by some to be more important as a poet than as a musician?

4. Name two important pieces by Paul Simon and two by Bob Dylan.

5. What type of pop music can be described as **song cycle**, and which pop group mentioned here has written and recorded two such works?

6. Who wrote and recorded *Dark Side of the Moon*? What does it represent?

7. In what way has Frank Zappa's music been criticized?

8. Name the composer of *Tubular Bells*. Why is it thought to be an important record?

9. What do you think is the main difference between progressive rock and the rock 'n' roll music of Bill Haley and Elvis Presley?

10. Name the three types of black music that have been popular in the 60s and 70s. What are the differences between them?

LISTENING
Elvis Presley *The 56 Sessions Vol. 1* RCA PL 42101
Beatles *1962–1966* Parlophone PCSP 717
   1967–1970 Parlophone PCSP 718
Bob Dylan *Greatest Hits* CBS 62847
   Blood on the Tracks CBS 69097
Simon and Garfunkel *Greatest Hits* CBS 69003
Rolling Stones *Big Hits, High Tide and Green Grass* Decca TXs 101
Jimi Hendrix *Are you experienced/Axis old as Love* Polydor 2683 011
The Who *Tommy* Track 2657 002
   Quadrophenia Track 2657 013
Pink Floyd *Dark Side of the Moon* Harvest SHVL 804
Frank Zappa *Apostrophe* Discreet K59201
Yes *Going for the One* Atlantic K50379
Mike Oldfield *Tubular Bells* Virgin V2001
Various Artists *Motown Gold* Motown STML 12003

106

COMPOSERS AND THEIR COUNTRIES

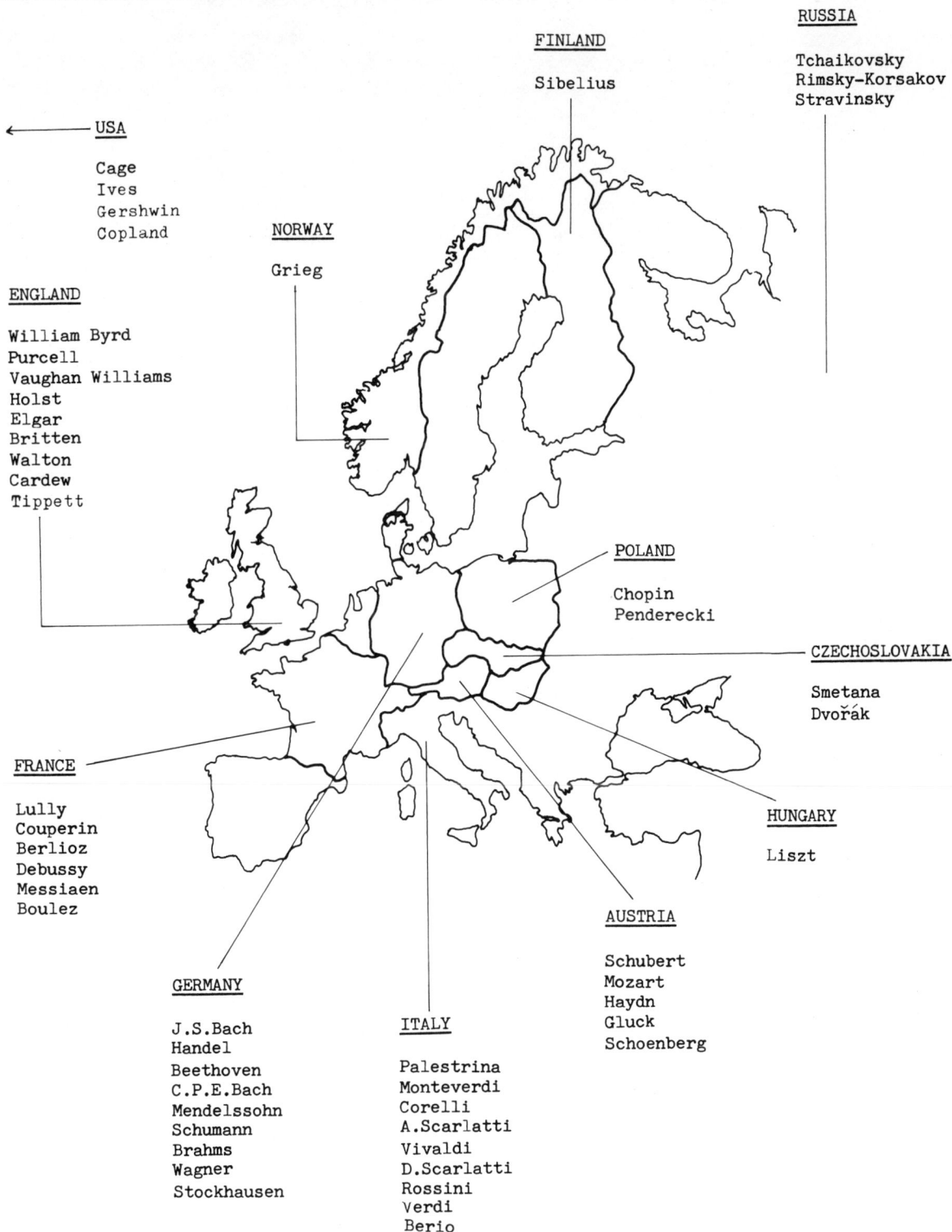

RUSSIA

Tchaikovsky
Rimsky-Korsakov
Stravinsky

FINLAND

Sibelius

USA

Cage
Ives
Gershwin
Copland

NORWAY

Grieg

ENGLAND

William Byrd
Purcell
Vaughan Williams
Holst
Elgar
Britten
Walton
Cardew
Tippett

POLAND

Chopin
Penderecki

CZECHOSLOVAKIA

Smetana
Dvořák

FRANCE

Lully
Couperin
Berlioz
Debussy
Messiaen
Boulez

HUNGARY

Liszt

AUSTRIA

Schubert
Mozart
Haydn
Gluck
Schoenberg

GERMANY

J.S.Bach
Handel
Beethoven
C.P.E.Bach
Mendelssohn
Schumann
Brahms
Wagner
Stockhausen

ITALY

Palestrina
Monteverdi
Corelli
A.Scarlatti
Vivaldi
D.Scarlatti
Rossini
Verdi
Berio

22 Important composers

J. S. BACH
Dates 1685–1750
Country Germany
Family Very musical. His ancestors were musicians and several of his sons became famous composers.
Most famous type of music Keyboard, church and orchestral.
Fame In his own time as an organist. Now thought of as one of the greatest composers of all time.
Famous pieces Keyboard: *48 Preludes and Fugues*
Orchestral: *Brandenburg concertos*
Church music: *St Matthew Passion; B minor Mass*
Organ music: *Toccata and Fugue in D minor*

LUDWIG VAN BEETHOVEN
Dates 1770–1827
Country Germany
Family Father was a musician.
Most famous types of music Symphonies, chamber music, piano sonatas, piano concertos. Wrote one opera: *Fidelio*.
Fame Famous in his life as a composer, and now recognized as one of the greatest composers ever.
Famous pieces Orchestral: All nine symphonies are very famous, especially numbers 3, 5 and 9.
Piano sonatas: 'Pathétique', 'Moonlight', 'Waldstein'. 'Appassionata'
Piano concerto: 'Emperor'
Violin concerto

HECTOR BERLIOZ
Dates 1803–1869
Country France
Family Son of a doctor.
Most famous type of music Orchestral programme music.
Fame Well known as conductor, composer, and critic; won a major compositional prize.
Famous pieces *Symphonie Fantastique*, programme work for orchestra
Te Deum, Requiem – large-scale choral works.
Opera: *The Trojans*

JOHANNES BRAHMS
Dates 1833–1897
Country Germany
Family Son of a musician.
Most famous type of music Orchestral.
Fame Well known and acclaimed when alive, and friendly with several other composers, including Schumann and Liszt
Famous pieces Four symphonies
German Requiem
Orchestral work: Academic Festival Overture
Concertos: Violin concerto, two piano concertos

BENJAMIN BRITTEN
Dates 1913–1976
Country England
Family Moderately well off.
Most famous type of music Operas, songs, choral music.
Fame A child prodigy, famous as a composer throughout his life – his

Hector Berlioz

Johannes Brahms

fame continues after his death. Co-founder of Aldeburgh Festival.
Famous pieces Opera: *Peter Grimes, The Turn of the Screw; Billy Budd*
Choral: *War Requiem*

FREDERICK CHOPIN
Dates 1810–1849
Country Poland
Family French father, Polish mother, both well educated.
Most famous type of music Piano music.
Fame Infant prodigy, famed as a performer throughout his life.
Famous pieces Polish dances: mazurkas, polonaises, waltzes.

AARON COPLAND
Dates 1900–
Country USA
Family From Brooklyn, New York.
Most famous type of music Ballets and symphonies.
Fame Has gained much recognition as a leading American composer since the war. Also known as a conductor, writer and lecturer.
Famous pieces Ballet: *Appalachian Spring; Billy the Kid*
Third symphony

ANTONIN DVOŘÁK
Dates 1841–1904
Country Czechoslovakia
Family Son of a village butcher.
Most famous type of music Orchestral.
Fame Helped to recognition by Smetana and Brahms, and secured a government grant, achieving much fame.
Famous pieces Symphony No. 9: 'From the New World'
Carnival concert overture
Slavonic Dances

EDWARD ELGAR
Dates 1857–1934
Country England
Family Son of a musician.
Most famous type of music Choral and orchestral.
Fame Recognized as the most important English composer of the day. Knighted in 1904.
Famous piece Choral: *Dream of Gerontius* (oratorio)
Orchestral: Enigma Variations, Symphonies Nos. 1 and 2

GEORGE FRIDERIC HANDEL
Dates 1685–1759
Country Germany, but moved to England in 1712.
Family Son of a barber-surgeon, who at first did not think it a good idea for his son to become a musician.
Most famous type of music In his day, oratorios and operas, but now the operas are much less well known than the oratorios.
Fame Very well known in his lifetime.
Famous pieces Oratorios: *Messiah, Israel in Egypt, Samson, Judas Maccabeus*
Orchestral: *Water Music; Fireworks Music*

FRANZ JOSEPH HAYDN
Dates 1732–1809
Family Very poor. Father an amateur musician, but no musical tradition in the family.
Most famous type of music Symphonies, chamber music.
Fame By old age, famous throughout Europe as a composer.
Famous pieces Symphonies: Surprise Symphony; London Symphonies; The 'Clock' symphony; The 'Toy' symphony
Oratorio: *The Creation*

ntonin Dvořák

eorge Frideric Handel

ranz Joseph Haydn

Felix Mendelssohn

Robert Schumann

FELIX MENDELSSOHN
Dates 1809–1847
Country Germany
Family Wealthy and cultured.
Most famous type of music Orchestral.
Fame Recognized as a gifted composer very early in life. Also known for popularizing the work of J. S. Bach, whose music at that time was largely unknown.
Famous pieces Orchestral overtures: *Midsummer Night's Dream; The Hebrides* (also called *Fingal's Cave*) Symphonies: The 'Scotch'; The 'Italian'
Oratorio: *Elijah*

WOLFGANG AMADEUS MOZART
Dates 1756–1791
Country Austria
Family Very musical.
Most famous type of music Symphonies, operas, piano sonatas, concertos.
Fame By 10 years old he had toured Europe as a pianist. His music was admired, but not always fully understood during his lifetime.
Famous pieces Operas: *Don Giovanni, The Magic Flute, The Marriage of Figaro*
Symphonies: Jupiter; G minor

HENRY PURCELL
Dates 1659–1695
Country England
Family Father a musician
Most famous type of music Theatre music and church music.
Fame Recognized as an important musician in his lifetime and employed in Westminster Abbey and Chapel Royal. Now regarded as one of the greatest English composers.

Famous pieces Opera: *Dido and Aeneas*
Stage music: *The Fairy Queen*

FRANZ SCHUBERT
Dates 1797–1828
Country Austria
Family Son of a school teacher, not very well off.
Most famous type of music Songs, chamber music and symphonies.
Fame Never achieved great public fame during his short life although well known by other artists and musicians.
Famous pieces Symphonies: the 'Unfinished'; The 'Great' C Major
Chamber music: 'Trout' Quintet
Songs: The 'Erl King'

ROBERT SCHUMANN
Dates 1810–1856
Country Germany
Family Son of a publisher – well educated.
Most famous type of music Piano music and songs.
Fame His piano music was made well known by his wife Clara who was a brilliant pianist. He was also well known as a critic.
Famous pieces Symphonies: Four, including No. 1 in B flat (The 'Spring') and No. 3 in E flat (The 'Rhenish')
Piano music: *Scenes of Childhood*;
Piano concerto
Song cycles: *Woman's Life and Love*

DMITRI SHOSTAKOVICH
Dates 1906–1975
Country Russia
Family No musical tradition in the family. But one of his sons has become a conductor.
Most famous type of music Symphonies.
Fame The most important Soviet

composer of his generation, although at various times during his career he was criticized by the authorities for writing music that was not representative of communist ideals.

Famous pieces 15 symphonies (including No. 7 'The Leningrad') 15 string quartets
Orchestral piece: *The Execution of Stepan Razin.*

JEAN SIBELIUS

Dates 1865–1957
Country Finland
Family Son of a doctor.
Most famous type of music Orchestral.
Fame Recognized as a great composer during his life, especially in his own country. In 1897 he was given a government grant for life.
Famous pieces Seven symphonies – especially Nos. 2, 5, and 7 Symphonic tone-poems: *Finlandia, Kalevala, Tapiola*

Jean Sibelius

IGOR STRAVINSKY

Dates 1882–1971
Country Russia, but moved to Paris, and then to USA.
Family Son of an opera singer.
Most famous type of music Music for ballet, symphonies, choral works.
Fame His ballet music made him famous, though was sometimes badly received. A major composer.
Famous pieces Ballets: *The Firebird; Petrushka; The Rite of Spring*
Opera: *The Rake's Progress*
Symphony: Symphony of Psalms

PETER ILICH TCHAIKOVSKY

Dates 1840–1893
Country Russia
Family Son of a mining engineer.
Most famous type of music Orchestral music, ballet music, opera.

Fame At first he showed few signs of musical ability but later became the first Russian composer to achieve fame outside his own country.
Famous pieces Symphonies: Nos. 4 (F minor) 5 (E minor) and 6 (B minor)
Ballet music: *Swan Lake; Sleeping Beauty; Nutcracker*
Opera: *Eugene Onegin*
Overtures: *Romeo and Juliet, 1812*
Two piano concertos, Violin concerto

RALPH VAUGHAN WILLIAMS

Dates 1872–1958
Country England
Family Son of a vicar, fairly well off.
Most famous type of music Church, vocal, orchestral, film music.
Fame A leading British composer.
Famous pieces Nine symphonies – including *A Sea Symphony* (No. 1), A vocal and orchestral work, and *A London Symphony* (No. 2)
Opera: *The Pilgrim's Progress*
Church music: Mass in G minor
Orchestral works: *The Wasps, Fantasia on a Theme of Thomas Tallis, Fantasia on Greensleeves*

RICHARD WAGNER

Dates 1813–1883
Country Germany
Family 9th child of a court clerk who died the year his son was born. Brought up by stepfather, an actor.
Most famous type of music Operas.
Fame Gradually recognized in his life time as a great composer (although at one time banned from Germany for taking part in a revolution).
Famous pieces Operas: *The Flying Dutchman; Tannhäuser; Lohengrin; The Ring* (consisting of *Rhinegold; The Valkyrie; Siegfried; Twilight of the Gods*); *Tristan and Isolde; The Mastersingers; Parsifal.*

SECTION 3

Some musical instruments

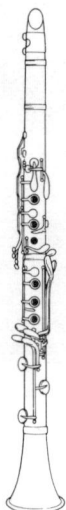

Clarinet

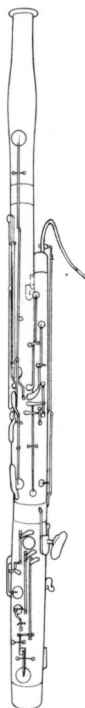

Bassoon

Arp A type of **synthesizer**, often used by pop groups.

Bass Either an electric bass guitar, as used in pop groups, or a double bass, if one is talking about jazz. If talking about the orchestral instrument it is normal to use the full term: **double bass**.

Bass clarinet A very large version of the B flat clarinet. A transposing instrument with a single reed. Pitch:

SOUNDS:

WRITTEN:

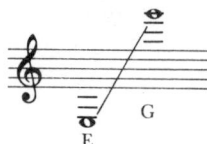

Bass drum A very large drum which gives a very deep sound. It is hit with a large soft headed stick. In a drum kit the stick is fitted to a foot pedal.

Bass guitar An electric guitar with four strings used for playing the bass line in pop music.

Bassoon A woodwind instrument over one metre long with a double reed. The instrument is in fact folded in half, and thus is really nearly three metres long, which enables it to play very low notes. Pitch:

Brass The name given to a group of instruments often found in symphony orchestras, including the cornet, French horn, trombone, trumpet, tuba.

Castanets A pair of small hollow pieces of wood, held in the hand. Used in Spanish dances, where the dancer holds and plays the castanets whilst dancing.

Cello The third largest member of the string family. It has four strings and is usually played with a bow. It is like a small version of the **double bass**. Pitch of the strings:

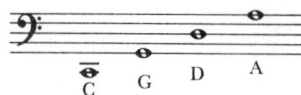

Clarinet A woodwind instrument about 60cm long, with a single reed, found in orchestras and jazz groups. It is a transposing instrument – the most common version being the B flat clarinet. It has a large number of holes and keys which give it a wide range of notes. Pitch:

WRITTEN:

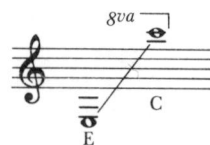

SOUNDS:

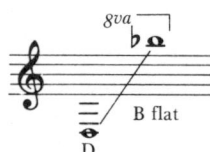

Cor anglais

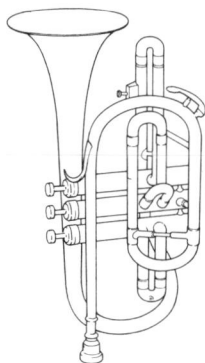

Cornet

Classical guitar A six-string non-electric guitar which is used for playing music other than folk or pop. It is like a folk guitar, but the strings are wider apart and are wound in nylon to give a softer tone.

Cor anglais A transposing woodwind instrument of the orchestra, rather like a large oboe. Many composers have used it for sad moments in their music. Pitch:

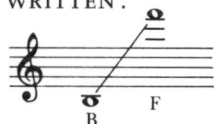

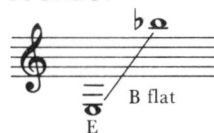

Cornet A transposing brass instrument with three valves. It is often found in brass bands and is used to play very quick pieces of music which it can handle well. Some composers have used it in the orchestra. Pitch:

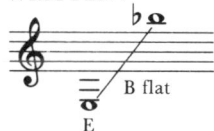

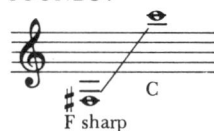

Cymbals A pair of cymbals consisting of two plates made of brass, which are either clashed together or hit with a stick. A wide variety of sounds can be made by hitting the cymbals in various ways on different parts of the plates. In the drum kit there is a pair of cymbals called a **hi-hat**. These are fitted to a foot pedal which when depressed bangs the cymbals together.

Double bass The largest member of the string family in the orchestra, with four strings. It plays the lowest notes of all the string instruments, either with a bow or plucked.

Pitch of the four strings WRITTEN:

sounding one octave lower.

Double bassoon The lowest of all the woodwind instruments. It is very similar to the bassoon, but is larger and therefore produces even lower notes. Pitch:

sounding one octave lower

Electric guitars Guitars with solid bodies which cannot produce sounds without being attached to an amplifier and speakers. There are two types – the **bass** guitar and the **lead** guitar (sometimes called the **rhythm** guitar). It is possible to change a non-electric guitar into an electric guitar by fitting a pickup under the strings of the guitar.

Electric instruments In recent years certain instruments have been prepared so that the sound is fed into an amplifier and then into a loudspeaker, in order to make it louder. Recent electric instruments include electric violins, harmonicas, guitars, and cellos.

Flute A woodwind instrument held horizontally. It has no reed. Its highest notes are produced by the player over-blowing (that is, blowing harder than usual) whilst

113

placing the fingers in the positions for producing the lower notes. Pitch:

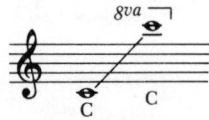

Folk guitar An acoustic (non-electric) guitar used to play folk music. It has six strings usually wound in steel rather than in nylon, and has a narrower neck than the classical guitar.

French horn A brass instrument with a tube wound round in a spiral, and three valves. The notes on the French horn sound a fifth lower than written. Pitch:

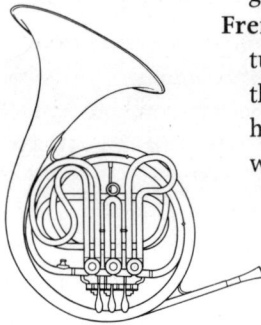

WRITTEN:

SOUNDS:

French horn

Glockenspiel A percussion instrument (often simply called a glock) made of a series of steel plates, laid out as a keyboard, the keys being struck with wooden hammers. Glocks come in various sizes, but the most common covers two and a half octaves.

Gong A large plate of metal with the edges turned back. It is usually hit with a padded stick, but in some modern pieces of music it is scraped or hit in special ways to produce unusual effects.

Guitar See **Bass guitar, Classical guitar, Electric guitar, Folk guitar, Lead guitar** and **Rhythm guitar.**

Hammond organ A type of electric organ made by the Hammond Company often used in dance bands and some pop groups.

Harp A large instrument whose strings

Oboe

are plucked by the player. It has seven pedals each of which can raise or lower each note by half a tone. The harp is a chromatic instrument, which means it can play all the notes obtainable on keyboard instruments such as the piano.

Harpsichord A keyboard instrument looking rather like a small grand piano, except that it often has two keyboards. The strings of the harpsichord are plucked by quills which are moved when a note is pressed down. This is different from a piano in which the strings are hit by hammers. The harpsichord is sometimes fitted with various stops which can vary the tone produced by the instrument.

Kettledrum See **Timpani**.

Lute A plucked instrument held like a guitar but with a pear-shaped body. The neck is shorter than that of a guitar, and the strings (which vary in number) are usually tuned in pairs.

Mouth organ A small instrument (often called a harmonica) which the player blows, or sucks. The front of the mouth organ contains a number of small holes and each one produces two notes – one when blown and one when sucked.

Oboe A small, straight, double-reeded woodwind instrument which has a bell shape at one end. It is the highest of the double-reeded orchestral instruments. Pitch:

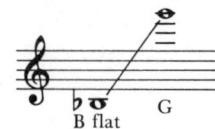

Organ A keyboard instrument into which wind is blown by bellows. Attached to the keyboard are a number of pipes – each pipe producing one pitch when wind is

blown through it. Tone is varied by means of stops, and usually several keyboards (including one operated by the feet called a pedal board) are provided so that different tone colours can be set up before one begins playing. Modern organs are now powered by electricity.

Percussion All percussion instruments have one thing in common – they are all played by the performer hitting them with a stick, or, (as with cymbals and castanets), hitting two of the instruments together. There are two types – *pitched* and *unpitched*. Those with pitch are able to produce a definite note, or series of notes, those without pitch cannot, and so are not tuned. Pitched percussion instruments include timpani, glockenspiels, xylophones, tubular bells and vibraphones. Unpitched percussion instruments include side, tenor, and bass drums, tambourines, triangles, cymbals, gongs and castanets.

Piano A keyboard instrument in which the keys are pressed down by the player, causing hammers to hit the strings. The volume can be controlled by the performer who depresses the keys harder in order to produce greater volume.

Piccolo A small flute with exactly the same fingering as the flute, but playing an octave higher. Like the flute it is a reedless woodwind instrument. Pitch:

WRITTEN:

8va

D   C

sounding one octave higher

Recorder A simple woodwind instrument not normally found in the orchestra. There are four types of recorder in use today – treble, descant, tenor and bass, the bass being the largest and deepest instrument.

Rhythm guitar An electric guitar, exactly the same as a lead guitar, but with the tone controls set slightly differently and used for playing chords rather than melodies.

Saxophone A single reeded metal instrument invented in the 19th century. Found in jazz and the works of some 20th-century composers of orchestral music.

Side drum A small drum used in the drum kit of a pop or jazz group, in the percussion section of the orchestra, and in marching bands. It is also known as a **snare drum**. 'Snares' are strings of wire-covered gut which, when tightened against the drum head, produce a rattling effect.

Strings The string section of the orchestra is one of the four main 'families' – along with the **brass, woodwind** and **percussion**. It consists of the violins, violas, cellos and double basses. Although some other instruments contain strings (such as the piano or harp) these instruments are not part of any particular family.

String bass A name used for the double bass, to distinguish it from an electric bass guitar.

Synthesizer This is the most complex of all musical instruments, an electronic device which is able to make an almost endless number of sounds, stretching above and below the normal range of human hearing. Synthesizers can produce various sounds which are put on tape for use in studios, and can also imitate orchestral instruments. To obtain

Saxophone

Piccolo

115

different effects, the sounds of non-electric instruments are often fed into the synthesizer and then 'treated' by the machine.

Synthi A type of synthesizer commonly found in small electronic music studios.

Tambourine A simple percussion instrument made of wood with parchment stretched over it and bells around the side. It is played by shaking or banging the parchment with the hand or fingers.

Tenor drum A drum similar in construction to a side drum, but larger, and with more depth between the top and bottom. Unlike the side drum, it is not fitted with snares.

Timpani Very large drums that can be tuned to play particular notes. The drums are shaped like bowls and made of copper. They are used in symphony orchestras where it is common for two or three sizes to be employed, each tuned to a different note. The range of pitch available for timpani is

for the larger drums:

E flat   B flat

for the smaller drums:

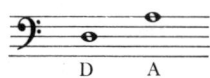
D   A

There are also medium-sized drums tuned between these ranges.

Transposing instruments A transposing instrument is one that is designed to produce a sound at a particular interval above or below the note written. Thus if a clarinet in B flat plays a note written as

C

the sound produced will in fact be:

B flat

One reason for this is that it enables a performer to play a number of instruments in one family without having to learn a new system of fingering for each instrument. The main transposing instruments of the orchestra are:

the **cor anglais** (which sounds a fifth lower than written);

the B flat **clarinet** (which sounds one tone lower than written); the **bass clarinet** which sounds a ninth (that is, an octave and one tone) lower than written;

the **trumpet**, which may be in B flat when it plays a tone lower than written; or A when it plays one and a half tones lower than written;

the **French horn** which sounds a fifth lower than written.

Triangle A small unpitched percussion instrument shaped like a triangle and hit with a metal beater.

Trombone An orchestral instrument also found in jazz bands; one of the brass family of instruments. The most common is the tenor trombone although tenor-bass and bass trombone are also used. It can be recognized because of its slide which is moved in and out to produce different fundamental (or bass) notes from which others are produced to give a full range of notes, by a technique called overblowing. Pitch: Tenor trombone

E   B♭

plus the notes

B flat   A   A flat   G

Timpani

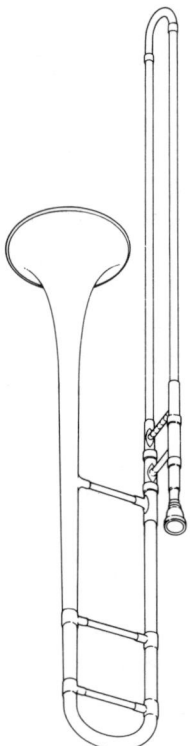

Trombone

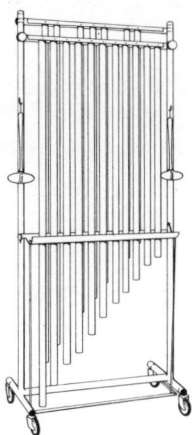

Tubular bells

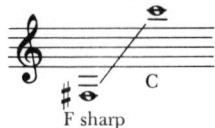

Violin

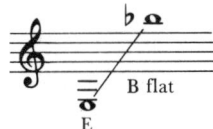

Viola

Trumpet A transposing brass instrument found in the orchestra and jazz bands. It has three valves. The player can blow with varying degrees of strength and move the valves in order to get a complete range of notes. Pitch:

Trumpet in B flat WRITTEN:

F sharp   C

SOUNDS:

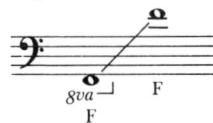

E   B flat

Tuba This is the lowest brass instrument of all usually found playing a simple bass accompaniment to the more active higher instruments. Pitch:

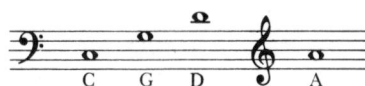

F   F

Tubular bells A set of usually eighteen metal tubes, suspended vertically. They cover one and a half octaves, and are struck with two wooden mallets. They are part of the pitched percussion section of the orchestra, and are often used to give the effect of church bells.

Vibraphone A large pitched percussion instrument rather like a glockenspiel, but with electrically-operated resonators under each note. They make the sound last longer and give a fuller effect. Also known by the shortened version of its name: **vibes.**

Viol A family of stringed instruments popular in the 15th-17th centuries. Played with a bow. The viols had flat backs and a fingerboard fitted with frets.

Viola The second smallest member of the string family. It is held under the chin, and, like the violin, is played with a bow or plucked. It has four strings which are tuned a fifth below the violin. Pitch of the strings:

C   G   D   A

Violin The smallest of the stringed instruments in the orchestra, having four strings. Usually played with a bow, but sometimes plucked. Like the viola, it is held under the chin when played. Pitch:

G   D   A   E

Woodwind One of the four families of instruments in the orchestra. The woodwind instruments are the **flute, piccolo, oboe, cor anglais, clarinet, bass clarinet, bassoon** and **double bassoon.**

Xylophone An instrument rather like a glockenspiel in the pitched percussion section of the orchestra, but made with wooden rather than metal plates, which are hit with beaters.

117

QUESTIONS 1. Which family of instruments contains the trombone?

2. Which guitar only has four strings?

3. What is the name of the large instrument with seven pedals and strings that are plucked by the player?

4. Which two transposing instruments play a fifth lower than written?

5. Which electronic instrument is the most complex instrument ever invented?

6. Name the four families of instruments of the orchestra.

7. Name two unpitched percussion instruments.

8. What is the name of the small instrument which has exactly the same fingering as the flute but plays an octave higher?

9. What is another name for a harmonica?

10. What is the name of the brass instrument with three valves which has a tube wound round in a spiral?

11. Which percussion instruments are used by Spanish dancers and played whilst they are dancing?

12. Name the lowest instrument in the woodwind family.

13. Name two types of acoustic guitar, and two types of electric guitar.

14. What types of drum might you find in a normal drum kit used by a pop group?

15. What is the name given to the very large drums found in the orchestra that can be tuned to different pitches?

16. Name four pitched percussion instruments.

17. Name the instruments in the string section of the orchestra. Which one can play the lowest notes?

18. Name the instrument that is rather like a guitar but which has a pear-shaped body and strings usually tuned in pairs.

19. Name a single reeded woodwind instrument.

20. Which instrument in the brass family plays the lowest notes?

SECTION 4

Some musical words

Accelerando Gradually get quicker.

Adagio Slow, but not as slow as **largo**.

Aleatoric music Music in which the composer does not tell the performer exactly what to do but leaves the decision as to what is to be played to chance. (The word comes from the Latin **alea** meaning 'dice'.)

Allegretto Quite quick but not as fast as **allegro**.

Allegro Quick and lively.

Allemande A dance movement from the classical suite in $\frac{4}{4}$ time played at a moderate speed.

Andante Flowing, but fairly slow.

Alto A low woman's voice, second line of music in four-part choral works – lower than the soprano line and higher than tenor. Also used in some families of instruments.

Aria A solo vocal piece often in *ternary* form, found in operas. 17th- and 18th-century operas are largely made up of arias alternating with recitative, but in recent times the number of arias has been much smaller.

Arco Play with the bow (used with violin, viola, cello or double bass, usually after a plucked passage).

Atonal Used to describe modern music which is not based on any key.

Bass The lowest man's voice, written on the lowest line of music in four-part choral works – below the tenor line. Also used in some families of instruments.

Basso continuo Italian term meaning 'continuous bass' or 'figured bass'. It consisted of a bass line with figures under or over it. From these the keyboard player (probably a harpsichordist) worked out which chords he should use to complete his part, since in the 17th and 18th centuries parts were rarely written out in full.

Binary form A piece in binary form has two parts. The second is a reply to the first. The piece often changes key in the middle and then goes back to the original key before the end. In the diagram below, 'A' is the first part, and 'B' is the second.

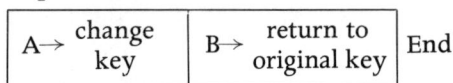

A→ change key	B→ return to original key	End

Blues A musical style from black America, generally rather slow and employing feelings of sadness and deprivation. Much pop music has been based on chord-progressions used in the blues. (See **Twelve-bar blues**.)

Bourrée French dance in $\frac{2}{4}$ time, often found in **suites** from the Baroque period.

Cantata A work for choir, soloist, or both, and often accompanied by an orchestra. Usually sacred.

Chamber music Music for two or more instruments (but rarely more than eight) in which each instrument plays its own individual part. Thus if two violins are included they will each have their own part to play.

Chromatic scale A scale in which the distance between one note and the next is always a semitone.

Chorus In opera this either means the choir or the music sung by the choir. It can also mean a part of a song that is repeated after each verse.

Classical This term is sometimes used for all 'serious' music, i.e. all Western music between 1550 and the present day, excluding pop, jazz, and folk. In music history, it refers to the music of the 18th century in which form and style were thought more important than the expression of the individual's feelings.

Coda A short section added on to the end of a piece in order to give a satisfactory conclusion.

Concerto A large-scale work in three movements in which the orchestra is contrasted with the playing of one or two solo instruments. In the work, the soloists sometimes play alone, sometimes with the orchestra, and are sometimes silent while the orchestra takes over.

Concerto grosso Orchestral music in which the orchestra is divided into two groups – a small section of, usually, string instruments, and the rest of the orchestra. (Plural: **concerti grossi**)

Continuo See **Basso continuo**.

Contrapuntal music See **Counterpoint**.

Counterpoint Music in two or more parts, in which each part has a melody line, and all these lines fit together in harmony. It is common for the parts to imitate each other, sometimes exactly, sometimes with variations. The adjective from 'counterpoint' is **contrapuntal**.

Country and western White American Folk music (mountain ballads, cowboy songs, religious music and work songs) from the Western and Central States. Usually played on stringed instruments, it is one of the ancestors of rock 'n' roll.

Courante A dance used as a movement in the classical suite, played in three-time.

Crescendo Gradually get louder. Often written:

Da capo or **D.C.** (It.) 'From the head'. This tells the performer to start again from the beginning of the piece, and is written above the staves.

Dal segno 'From the sign'. This instructs the performer to return to the sign (usually marked 𝄋). The music is then repeated, usually either to a **fine** or to a double bar with a pause sign.

Development The middle section of a piece in **sonata form**.

Diminuendo Gradually get softer. Often written:　　　　The opposite to crescendo.

Dominant The fifth note of a scale. In the key of C major it is G. The dominant chord is the chord built on the fifth note of the scale.

Duet A piece for two performers.

Electronic music Music created either from electronic instruments themselves or by treating the sounds of conventional instruments electronically. Instruments are sometimes recorded on tape and then the tape itself is altered. The most important electronic instrument is the synthesizer.

Episode Refers either to passages in a **rondo** which occur between statements of the main theme, or to passages in a **fugue** which provide a link between appearances of the fugue subject.

Exposition The first section of a piece

in **sonata form**.

f Loud (from the Italian **forte**).

ff Very loud (from the Italian **fortissimo**).

fff Very loud indeed.

fz Suddenly loud.

Figured bass Another term for **basso continuo**.

Fine Italian word for 'end'.

Forte Loud. 'f' (above) is short for **forte**.

Fugue A very complicated type of **contrapuntal** writing which usually follows strict rules about how each part should appear and fit in with all the other parts. The most famous fugues appear in *48 Preludes and Fugues* for keyboard by J. S. Bach.

Gavotte A French dance sometimes found in a Baroque suite, written in $\frac{2}{4}$ or $\frac{4}{4}$ time.

Gigue or **Jig** English dance, used as last movement in a Baroque suite in binary form, usually full of triplet figures.

Grave (It.) Slowly and solemnly.

Harmonic progression A series of chords coming one after the other.

Improvise To play without notation, making up the music as one goes along.

Indeterminacy In music, a situation where the performer is allowed to make the decision as to which part of the score to play, or in what order the various parts of the score should be played.

LH Play with the left hand – found in keyboard music.

Largo Very slow, dignified and broad in style.

Leading-note Seventh note of a scale. In the key of C major it is B.

Legato Play smoothly. Opposite of **staccato**.

Leitmotive Short melody used to represent an event, character or action, usually in opera. First introduced by Wagner.

Lento Slow, but usually not quite as slow as **largo**.

Lied (Ger.) A song – particularly used in the plural, **Lieder**, and generally refers to songs of the 19th-century German romantic composers, including Schubert and Brahms.

mf Fairly loud (from the Italian **mezzoforte**).

mp Fairly soft (from the Italian **mezzo piano**).

Madrigal A fairly short secular part-song, fashionable in England in the late 16th and early 17th centuries, and Italy in the 14th–17th centuries.

Mass A service used by the Catholic church. The mass is divided into six sections and is set to music for choir or choir and soloists. A famous example is the B Minor Mass by J. S. Bach.

Mediant The third note of a scale. In the key of C major it is E.

Minuet and trio The minuet, originally a 16th-century French dance, was, in the 18th century, usually combined with a second piece called a trio. Both pieces are in two sections. Each section is repeated, and the second usually contains a repeat of the opening theme of the first. The minuet is usually repeated once more after the trio, so the whole movement is in **ternary form**. Both Haydn and Mozart used this form a great deal, usually as the third movement of a four-movement symphony, quartet, or sonata.

Modes The system of scales which was commonly used in composition until the 17th century, when it was replaced by the major and minor scales. To play a mode on a piano, start on any white note (except B) and play the next seven white notes above it in ascending order. You will play a different mode for each white note you start on. The mode starting on C (the Ionian mode) is the same as the scale of C major.

Modulation Changing from one key to another during a piece of music.

Moderato Moderate speed, neither fast nor slow.

Molto Much or very, as in **molto allegro**, very fast.

Motet Sacred vocal composition. The term has been used in all periods since the 13th century.

Movement A movement is part of a larger piece of music such as a **symphony, sonata,** or **concerto.** A symphony, for example, may be divided into four (sometimes more or less) major sections, separated from each other by a short pause. Each section is a movement.

Music drama A term used by Wagner to describe his large-scale operatic works from *The Ring* onwards.

Opus Latin word meaning 'work'. When a composer has written many works they are numbered so that they can be referred to easily. An opus number can refer to one piece or several pieces together, in which case each piece has its own particular number after the opus number. Beethoven's 'Moonlight' Sonata (for piano) is known as Opus 27 No. 2.

Oratorio A large work with solo singers, choir, and orchestra based on a religious theme, but without any stage action. One of the most famous is *Messiah* by Handel.

Overture Either a piece for orchestra which comes before an oratorio or an opera, or an orchestral piece which is complete in itself, and written to be played in a concert (and therefore sometimes called a 'concert overture'). A famous example of the first kind of overture is that to Wagner's *Flying Dutchman. Fingal's Cave* by Mendelssohn is a well known concert overture.

Opera A large scale dramatic work in which some or all of the words are sung, with the singers also acting out the roles on stage, accompanied by an orchestra. Operatic composers include Mozart, Wagner and Verdi. Wagner preferred to describe his later works as **music dramas.**

p Soft (short for the Italian **piano**).

pp Very soft (short for the Italian **pianissimo**).

ppp Very soft indeed.

Passion A setting to music of the story of the crucifixion of Christ taken from one of the four Gospels.

Piano An Italian word meaning soft, often abbreviated to 'p'. Also the short name for the keyboard instrument, the pianoforte, so called because it can play soft and loud.

Più mosso Quicker.

Pizzicato Plucked. In music for string instruments, it shows that the notes are not to be played with the bow, but plucked with the fingers.

Plainsong An early type of church music in which there was one vocal line and no accompaniment. The rhythm of the chanting reflected the rhythms of speech, and so there was no regular pulse or time signature in plainsong.

Prelude An introduction.

Prepared piano A piano in which objects have been placed in order to change the sound of certain notes when they are played. John Cage has written several works for prepared piano.

Presto Very quick.

Programme music Music that is written in order to convey certain images to the listener (Mendelssohn's overture *Fingal's Cave*, for example). Berlioz's *Symphonie Fantastique*, was inspired by romantic episodes in the composer's life and could be called a 'programme symphony'.

Quartet A piece for four voices or instruments, or the group performing it.

Quintet As with quartet (above) but for five voices or instruments.

RH Play with the right hand (found in keyboard music).

Rallentando Slow down gradually.

Recapitulation The third section of a piece in sonata form.

Recitative Part of an opera or oratorio which links the arias and choruses. The singer often describes the plot in the recitative. It is often written in the short form RECIT.

Requiem A setting to music of the Mass for the dead.

Ritardando Gradually get slower. It is sometimes written RIT. for short.

Ritenuto (It.) 'Held back'. Tells the performer to play slightly slower (immediately, not gradually) in the following bars. Often confused with **ritardando**.

Romantic music This term is used to describe the music from the 19th-century composed by such people as Schubert, Brahms, Chopin, Mendelssohn, Liszt, Schumann, and Tchaikovsky.

Rondo A form of music with the following organization:
1. Theme
2. Episode
3. Theme (repeat of section 1)
4. Episode
5. Theme (repeat of section 1)

6. Coda

There can be as many episodes as the composer wishes to have, but each one is different. The coda rounds off the whole piece.

Rhythm 'n' blues A type of black music that combines elements of blues and jazz.

sf (Short for the Italian **sforzando**.) Play this note or chord louder than the others around it, i.e. accent it.

Sarabande Movement from a Baroque suite in binary form, usually in $\frac{3}{4}$ time.

Scherzando Light and quick.

Scherzo A light quick piece that replaced the **minuet** as a movement in symphonies by some composers.

Septet A piece written for seven voices or instruments, or the group performing it.

Serial composition A method of **atonal** composition usually based on a carefully worked out row of twelve different notes, called a **series**. In the piece, the relationships between each consecutive pair of notes are explored. The series itself can be used backwards, or upside-down (inverted), or both, i.e. in four different ways altogether, and can start on any note of the **chromatic scale**. The method was invented by Schoenberg in the early part of this century.

Series See **Serial composition**.

Sextet A piece written for six voices or instruments, or the group performing it.

Sonata A piece normally for one instrument, generally in three or four movements. Beethoven wrote 32 piano sonatas.

Sonata form The form that the first movement of a sonata, symphony, or quartet often takes. It is sometimes called 'first movement' form

(although it can be found in other movements too.)

Sonata form (or first movement form) has the following sections:

1. *Exposition* (containing all the main musical ideas of the piece) presented in two contrasting keys.
2. *Codetta* (ending the exposition).
3. *Development* (in which some of the musical ideas from the exposition are developed).
4. *Recapitulation* (which contains much of the exposition, repeated but usually all in the same key).
5. *Coda*.

The form is set out graphically below.

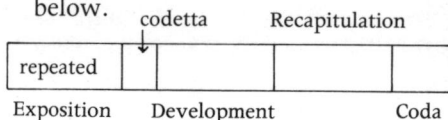

	codetta	Recapitulation	
repeated			
Exposition	Development		Coda

Song cycle A collection of songs connected together through the story that they tell, or a common idea. Schubert wrote some famous song cycles including *The Maid of the Mill* and *The Winter's Journey*.

Soprano A high woman's voice, the highest voice part in vocal music, above the alto. Also used to describe the instrument in a family of instruments with the highest pitch – for example, a soprano saxophone.

Spatial effects Effects obtained by placing the performers or groups of performers some distance from each other, to be found in some avant-garde compositions. Some choral and instrumental music in 16th-century Italy made use of spatial effects by placing various groups of voices or instruments in the separate galleries of such a cathedral as St. Mark's, Venice.

Staccato The notes are to be played short and detached.

String quartet A piece of music written for two violins, viola and cello, or simply those four instruments and their players.

Strophic form The simplest form of song in which each verse of the poem has the same music.

Subdominant Fourth note of a scale. In the key of C major it is F.

Submediant Sixth note of a scale. In the key of C major it is A.

Suite A collection of instrumental pieces played one after the other. In the baroque suite the pieces were all dances (such as **allemande, courante, sarabande, gigue, bourrée, gavotte,** and **minuet**).

Supertonic Second note of a scale. In the key of C major it is D.

Symphony A piece of music for orchestra. Different composers have written symphonies in a variety of ways, but many have adopted the following format:

1st movement: In sonata form, usually quite fast

2nd movement: Slow

3rd movement: Scherzo, or minuet and trio

4th movement: Finale, often a rondo or in sonata form. Usually quick and light.

Haydn, Mozart and Beethoven were all great symphonists.

Symphonic poem See **Tone poem**.

Tenor A man who has a high vocal range. The tenor part is written on the third line down in four-part choral works, lower than the alto part, but higher than the bass. Also sometimes used to describe one instrument in a family.

Ternary form A form in three parts in which the last part is the same as the first. In the middle part there is often a change to another key. It is shown graphically on the next page:

1st section	2nd section	1st section
A	B	A
	usually based on different key	repeated

Theme and variations In this form a theme (often in **binary form**) is played first and then a series of variations on the theme are played one after the other. The variations may change the speed, melody, harmony and so on, but must still be related to the original in some way.

Timbre The quality of musical sound itself, which distinguishes, for example, the sound of the oboe from that of the flute.

Tone poem or **Symphonic poem** An orchestral work in one movement which depicts an event, or relates to a poem, painting etc. It is thus a type of **programme music**.

Tonic The first note of a scale. In the scale of C major it is C.

Tremolo Rapid up and down movement by a bow on a string instrument.

Trio A work for three instruments or voices or the group performing it.

Tutti A piece or section where everyone plays. Used in concertos to show that this part is for the full orchestra and not just the soloist.

Twelve-bar blues A simple chord sequence often used in pop music, based on the traditional blues song. The first line of the song is repeated with a different-chord pattern underneath, and this is answered by the third line of the song. If the blues is to be played in E major the chord sequence will be:

E major (4 bars)	First line of melody
A major (2 bars)	} First line repeated
E major (2 bars)	
B7 (1 bar)	
A major (1 bar)	} Last line of melody
E major (1 bar)	
B7 (1 bar)	

The piece *Catherine's Blues* below is an instrumental 12-bar blues. A group might play the verse through once or twice before starting to add their own variations and gradually change the melody. However, the chord sequence would remain the same throughout. You'll notice that the third note of the scale of E major is often lowered a semitone (G sharp going down to G). The same happens with the 7th note (D sharp lowered to D). Also where the chord indicated is A, the 3rd and 7th note of the key of A major are lowered on occasion (C sharp to C, and G sharp to G). This procedure is very common in blues.

Variations See **Theme and variations**.

Vivace Lively.

Whole-tone scale Six-note scale in which the interval between one note and the next is always one tone. There are two whole-tone scales:

1. A B C sharp D sharp F G

2. A sharp C D E F sharp G sharp

Catherine's Blues   by Tony Attwood

125

QUESTIONS   1. The first note of a scale is called the tonic. What is the fourth note called?

2. What was the term that Wagner used for his major stage works?

3. What words would you find in a score to indicate to a violinist that he or she should a) play with the bow and b) pluck the string?

4. What is the name given to a piece of music played by two violins, a viola and a cello?

5. If a piece of music opens with one section, then has a contrasting section and then a repeat of the first section, what is the form called?

6. What is the name of the scale that contains six different notes with the distance between each note and the next always the same?

7. What is the name given to music in which the composer leaves some decisions as to what is to be played to the performer?

8. Give the name of two forms of sacred vocal composition.

9. What is the difference between a sonata and sonata form?

10. What is the name of the short section added to the end of a piece in sonata form in order to round the piece off?

11. What is the Italian word that means 'slow down gradually'?

12. What are the names given to the four lines in a four part vocal work? Which is the highest and which is the lowest?

13. Which English dance is often used as the last movement in a Baroque suite?

14. What is the technical term that means a change from one key to another in a piece of music?

15. In a concerto a word might be written in the score to show that everyone plays, rather than just the soloist. What is that word?

16. Before the system of major and minor keys was in common use another system of scales was used by composers. What was that system called?

17. What is the name given to the large scale choral and orchestral works that are based on religious subjects, and have a similar style to that of opera, except that there is no acting?

18. What is the name given to a sacred work for choir, soloists, or both, and often accompanied by an orchestra?

19. What Italian words indicate that the player must return to the sign and repeat the passage from there?

20. Name the Italian words for a) fairly loud, b) loud, c) fairly soft, d) soft.

Examination questions

The following questions are very similar to those set by various C.S.E. examining boards in recent years. They relate to all sections of this book except the theory of music.

1. Which composer was born in Germany but moved to England and is now best remembered for his oratorios?
2. Who wrote a) the Italian Symphony, b) New World Symphony, c) the Unfinished Symphony?
3. Which is the lowest voice: bass, soprano, tenor or alto?
4. How many movements does a classical symphony normally have?
5. Which English city is noted for its piano competition?
6. With which artistic movement is Debussy associated?
7. Name two instruments which cannot play notes of a definite pitch.
8. Who wrote the 'Pomp and Circumstance' marches?
9. With which instrument is Chopin usually associated?
10. A fugue is a **contrapuntal** piece of music. What is the meaning of **counterpoint**? Name a composer who wrote fugues.
11. Would you associate Mozart with the Baroque, Classical, Romantic, or Avant-Garde?
12. Describe the musical life of Beethoven and name some of his important works.
13. What is **aleatory** music? Name a composer who has written music in this style.
14. What is rock 'n' roll? Name any performers you know who have been associated with it.
15. Name any opera by Benjamin Britten.
16. In what musical form would you expect to find a) allemande, courante, sarabande and gigue, b) recitative?
17. Name one composition by a) Vaughan Williams, b) Edward Elgar.
18. Name a composer you would associate with each of the following: a) Lied, b) Leitmotive.
19. Name two transposing instruments in the symphony orchestra.
20. What do you consider to be the most interesting trends in pop music today? Give reasons for your choice.
21. What is serial music? Name a composer who used this technique.
22. Explain the following: a) exposition, b) minuet and trio.
23. Write briefly about any symphony concert, opera, ballet or recital that you have recently attended.
24. Write briefly about any two modern performers who also compose all their own material.
25. Who is John Cage? Describe his contribution to music.
26. Write a short account of music festivals in Britain.

27. If you were invited to take part in a *Desert Island Discs* programme what records would you take with you, and why?

28. What are the main differences between an oratorio and an opera? Name a composer of each type of work and one of his compositions in this form.

29. Put the following in historical order: Berlioz, Bach, Palestrina, Beethoven.

30. What is a tone-poem? Give an example.

31. Name any three composers who are alive today, and write very briefly about their work.

32. Name and describe any two brass instruments.

33. Which note of the scale is the sub-dominant?

34. Which instrument would you associate with the continuo part in Baroque music?

35. Put the following in historical order: Neo-romanticism, Romanticism, Avant-garde, Baroque, Classicism.

36. Name a transposing woodwind instrument.

37. How does the trombone differ from other brass instruments?

38. How and where did opera first begin?

39. What are the movements of a classical symphony? Describe the structure of any one of the movements in detail.

40. What is the difference between chamber music and orchestral music?

41. What is the difference between a concerto grosso, and a classical concerto? Name one composer associated with each type of concerto.

42. Compare the music of any two well known pop groups. State which you prefer and why.

43. What is a) aleatory music, b) electronic music, c) the whole-tone scale?

44. In what way are the flute and piccolo different from other woodwind instruments?

45. What sort of works are the *Barber of Seville* and *William Tell*? Who wrote them?

46. What is the meaning of the term 'opus'?

47. What sort of guitar plays the lowest notes in a pop group?

48. Explain the difference between binary form and ternary form.

49. What is the difference between an acoustic guitar and an electric guitar?

50. What is the main difference between a glockenspiel and a xylophone?